Dyer White Elderkin

Genealogy of the Elderkin family with intermarriages

Also, an appendix, containing aa few of the author's original articles on theories of science, pathology and theology

Dyer White Elderkin

Genealogy of the Elderkin family with intermarriages
Also, an appendix, containing aa few of the author's original articles on theories of science, pathology and theology

ISBN/EAN: 9783337884864

Printed in Europe, USA, Canada, Australia, Japan

Cover: Foto ©ninafisch / pixelio.de

More available books at **www.hansebooks.com**

GENEALOGY

—OF THE—

ELDERKIN FAMILY

WITH INTERMARRIAGES.

CONTAINING FAMILY RECORDS FROM JOHN IST, WHO CAME FROM ENGLAND IN A. D. 1637 AND LOCATED IN MASSACHUSETTS, THROUGH TEN GENERATIONS TO 1886; WITH BIOGRAPHICAL SKETCHES OF NEARLY ALL AND PRESENT ADDRESS OF THE LIVING ADULT MEMBERS OF THE FAMILY. ALSO,

AN APPENDIX,

CONTAINING A FEW OF THE AUTHOR'S ORIGINAL ARTICLES ON THEORIES OF SCIENCE, PATHOLOGY AND THEOLOGY.

PREFACE.

IN presenting this work on Genealogy to the relatives and friends of the Elderkin family my motives were entirely superior to any money interest. For many years I have had an unceasing desire to know the origin, progress, and mental and moral standing of our people. In them I had observed a class of uniform characteristic elements which, on investigation, are found to extend through the whole line of Ten Generations. To know why and how these peculiar traits of character can be held intact through so many intermarriages is a matter of interest to every thinking mind. A retrospective view of the noble acts and deeds of one's ancestors has a tendency to inspire a spirit of emulation. A knowledge of the importance of marrying into families of equal breed, blood and grade of physical, mental and moral development cannot be too strongly impressed upon the minds of the young. Wherever there is a cross into a lower class of people the children suffer a loss in some respect. Purity of blood from scrofula and consumption is a matter not to be overlooked any more than intellectuality, education, honesty, energy, industry, economy, morality and humanity; all of which combine to make a great and good person. A careful study of characters described in this work, it is hoped, will have a tendency to guide the feet of the young into paths of peace and prosperity; to encourage the middle aged to hold fast to their integrity and manhood, and the aged to pass down in peace and quietude to the final resting place of all.

These and other considerations to be found in this book prompted me to spend most of my time for three years to collect and compile the contents of this work for my children and your children and their children so long as paper and binding will hold together.

The older portion of the biographical sketches and family records was obtained by Wm. L. Weaver, of Willimantic, Ct., and furnished by Mrs. Fanny Elderkin, widow of Noble S. Elderkin, of Potsdam, St. Lawrence county, N.Y. Mrs. Jane E. Leffingwell, of Dansville, N.Y., and Miss Mary Anne Roberts, of 690 West Monroe street, Chicago, Ill., contributed largely to the stock of facts. I am also indebted to W. J. Brewster, Hannibal, N. Y.; Miss Harriet N. Elderkin, Ashville, N. Y.; Henry A. Jackson, proprietor of the Parcels House, Kirksville, Adair county, Mo.; H. A. Brewster, 395 Roberts street, St. Paul, Minn., and others for valuable information.

D. W. E.

GENEALOGY

OF THE

ELDERKIN FAMILIES

OF THE UNITED STATES OF AMERICA.

Compiled by Dyer White Elderkin, A. D. 1884.

CHAPTER I.

John Elderkin, the ancestor of the family, the progenitor of all who bear the name in this country, was born in England about 1612. He came to New England, and is first heard of at Lynn, Mass., in 1637. In 1641 he was at Dedham, Mass.; at Reading, Mass., in 1646; at Providence, R. I., in 1648; and at New London, Ct., in 1651. At all these places, it is said, he built a corn mill; and at New London a church. In 1663 he moved to Norwich, Ct., about four years after the settlement of that place, where he built the first mill and church erected in that town. In 1664 he moved to Killingworth, Conn., where he also built a mill on the Manunkatesk river. His lot there he sold to Wm. Wellman February 25th, 1666, and his corn mill to Thomas Stevens October 13th, 1671. He then returned to Norwich, where he died June 13th, 1687, aged 75 years. His life was an active and useful one, and he was evidently a man of energy and ability. His first wife's given name was Abigail; when and where married, and date of her death, is unknown. His second marriage was to Mrs. Elizabeth (Drake) Gaylord, daughter of John Drake and widow of Wm. Gaylord, of Windham,

Conn., March 1st, 1660. She died at Norwich June 8th, 1716, aged 95 years.

SECOND GENERATION—CHILDREN BY FIRST WIFE.

NAMES.	BORN.	MARRIED TO.	DATE OF MAR.	DIED.
1 Abigail.	Sept. 13, 1641.			
2 Hannah.		Richard Handy.	(Had one son,	
3 —— ——		Daniel Comestock.	Richard).	

CHILDREN BY SECOND WIFE.

NAMES.	BORN.	MARRIED TO.	DATE OF MAR.	DIED
1 Ann.	Jan., 1661.			
2 John 2d.	April, 1664.	Abigail Fowler.	—— ——, 1685.	March, 1714.
		2d, Han'h Coleman	Aug. 16, 1720.	
3 Bashaw.	Nov., 1665.			
4 James.	March, 1670.		(Died at Wind-	April 26, 1698.
5 Joseph.	Dec., 1672.		ham, Conn.)	

JOHN ELDERKIN, 2d, was married twice; first to Abigail Fowler, probably daughter of William Fowler, of Milford, in 1685; she died March, 1714. Married second wife, widow, Hannah Coleman, August 16, 1720. He bought the mill, at Killingworth, of the heirs of Thomas Stevens, 1702, and sold it to John Brown in 1704. The place and date of his death is not known.

THIRD GENERATION—CHILDREN BY FIRST WIFE.

NAMES.	BORN.	MARRIED TO.	DATE OF MAR.	DIED.
1 Abigail.	April 20, 1693.			
2 John 3d.	May 7, 1694.	Susannah Baker.	Aug. 26, 1714.	Feb. 27, 1737.
3 Benjamin.	Sept. 15, 1695.			April, 1699.
4 James,	Nov. 16, 1699.	Phœbe Lee.	June, 1722.	
5 Margaret.	Nov., 1700.			
6 Jedediah.	Nov. 7, 1701.			
7 Judith.	March 8, 1704.			

SECOND GENERATION—Joseph Elderkin, son of John 1st, born at Norwich December 27th, 1672. Married Deborah Brockway July 27th, 1703.

THIRD GENERATION—THEIR CHILDREN.

NAMES.	BORN.	MARRIED TO.	DATE OF MAR.	DIED.
1 Joseph.	—— —, 1707.			
2 Benjamin.	April 14, 1711.			
3 Elizabeth.	Aug. 27, 1717.			
4 Jeptha.	May 2, 1719.			
5 Deborah.	May, 1721.			

THIRD GENERATION—John Elderkin 3d, born May 7, 1694; died February 27, 1737. He was of Norwich. Married Susannah Baker, August 26, 1714.

FOURTH GENERATION—THEIR CHILDREN.

NAMES.	BORN.	MARRIED TO.	DATE OF MAR.	DIED.
1 Abigail.	Sept. 29, 1715.			
2 Jedediah 2d.	— —, 1717.	Anne Wood.	Aug. 31, 1741.	March 3, 1793.
3 John 4th.	Feb. 3, 1719.	Rebecca Allen.		
4 Joshua.	Oct. 30, 1720.	(Settled in Windam, had family).		
5 Susannah.	Aug. 12, 1722.			

THIRD GENERATION—James Elderkin, of Norwich, son of John 2d, married Phœbe Lee, June, 1722. Perhaps the same James married Betty Waterman August 31st, 1744, and had the following:

FOURTH GENERATION—CHILDREN BY SECOND WIFE.

NAMES.	BORN.	MARRIED TO.	DATE OF MAR.	DIED.
1 James.	Dec. 11, 1745.			
2 Betty.	Feb. 28, 1748.			
3 Rodolphus.	Oct. 4, 1750.			Mar. 29, 1753.
4 Louisa.	Dec. 22, 1752.			
5 Louisa 2d.	March 3, 1754.			
6 Cynthia.	March 3, 1757.			
7 Kadesh.	Dec. 14, 1758.			
8 Ahira	June 19, 1761.			
9 Annath.	Aug. 23, 1763			
10 Amanda.	Sept. 10, 1765.			

THIRD GENERATION—Joseph Elderkin, son of Joseph, born 1707. Married Mary Story, April 28, 1731.

FOURTH GENERATION—THEIR CHILDREN.

NAMES.	BORN.	MARRIED TO.	DATE OF MAR.	DIED.
1 Rachel.	March 6, 1732.			
2 Mary.	Dec. 9, 1736.			
3 James.	Oct. 19, 1739.	Twins		
4 Elizabeth.	Oct. 19, 1739.			
5 John.	April 23, 1745.			
6 Jemima.	July 23, 1747.			
7 Japtha.	May 19, 1750.			
8 Joseph 3d.	Sept. 15, 1753.			
9 Frederick.	Dec. 25, 1756.			
10 Rowminer.	Sept. 20, 1759.			

CHAPTER II.

Colonel Jedediah Elderkin was, as we have seen, the son of John Elderkin 3d. He was born at Norwich in 1717. He was married in Norwich, where his first child was born. He is first mentioned in Windham, Conn., records in December, 1744, and before September, 1745, he had removed from Norwich and settled in the town of Windom. His first purchase was of Gidion Bingham, who sold him two tracts of land, one on the east side of the town street, down town, and the other west of Shetucket river, December, 1744. No mention is made of a house on either tract, but we presume from the price paid (£600) that there was a house on the town street lot. Colonel Elderkin, if he lived in that part of the town at first, as seems probable, afterwards removed up town and owned and lived and died in the house now owned (1865) and occupied by Wm. Swift, Esq. Colonel Elderkin, we presume, was in the practice of law before he settled in Windham. He evidently stood high as an advocate, for his practice rapidly increased until it was quite extensive.

Windham, Conn., when Col. Elderkin settled in the town had been the county seat for some twenty years, and was then a place of considerable local importance. Colonel Elderkin and Colonel Dyer were unquestionably the leading lawyers in Eastern Connecticut, and their fame was not confined to their own section. Colonel Elderkin was about four years the senior of Colonel Dyer. During the revolution, in which both bore an honorable part, their views fully coincided on the important questions involved in that great struggle for American freedom. They were next door neighbors and personal friends. We have understood they often traveled together while journeying to fulfill their engagements, or attend to their official duties. In 1769 Colonel Elderkin, with Colonel Dyer, was appointed agent of the Susquehanna Land Company, and they went to Philadelphia to open negotiations for the settlement of the controversy respecting the Wyoming lands. Colonel Elderkin took but little part in town affairs, and his name is seldom mentioned in the records until 1767, when he was appointed Chairman of an important committee raised to take into consideration the state of the country and to promote industry, economy, manufactures, etc.; in other words, to consider whether the town would agree to the non-importation scheme started in Boston. The committee was appointed the 7th day of December, 1767, and on the 10th of January, 1768, made their report, drawn, we presume, by Colonel Elderkin, which fully endorsed the scheme, and pledged the members and the people of the town not to buy or sell, or use in their families, a great variety of imported articles, which were enumerated.

Colonel Elderkin was appointed Justice of the Peace in 1756, and continued by annual appointment until 1791, a period of thirty-five years, a length of time almost without a parallel. The office in his day was one of honor and importance. Colonel Elderkin was first chosen a member of the General Assembly from Windham in the Spring of 1751, and was chosen repeatedly afterwards until 1785, when he was elected for the last time. His name appears as a member in seventeen different years, and we find he attended thirty-five different sessions within that time. He was a member in 1774, 1775, 1776, 1779, 1780 and 1783, some of the most eventful years of the Revolution. Our account of the services rendered by Colonel Elderkin during the Revolution will be very meagre, but strictly reliable, as it is derived almost wholly from the State records.

At the March Session of the General Assembly in 1775, Jedediah Elderkin, Esq., was commissioned Colonel of the

Fifth Regiment of Connecticut Militia, and Experience Storrs, Esq., of Mansfield, was appointed Lieutenant-Colonel. This was an Eastern Regiment. This appointment gave Mr. Elderkin his military title. It does not appear, however, that he was ever on active duty.

His services were more needed in other quarters than in the field. December 9th, 1776, it was reported that Colonel Elderkin and Lieutenant Storrs were not in fit condition to march with the Fifth Regiment and the command was given to Major Brown. Colonel Elderkin was one of the first Committee of Safety, organized in 1775, and was often a member afterwards. November 2d, 1775, he was appointed by the Governor and Council of Safety, with Major Dawes, of Boston, then of Norwich, to view the harbor of New London and report places suitable to fortify. He visited New London, and on the 15th made a lengthy report. It was found impossible to procure an engineer, and Major Dawes declined the service. Colonel Elderkin therefore repaired to New London alone and examined the localities about the city, in company with some of the citizens, and after consulting with those best informed, gave the result of his observations and inquiries. The report is a clear and definite statement of his views on the importance and feasibility of fortifying the approaches of the harbor, and he names the island, or point, called Mamacock, Winthrop's Point, and Groton Hill, opposite New London, as places important to fortify. He gives a description of these localities, with heights and distances, and his opinion in regard to how and in what manner they should be fortified, with as much particularity as a topographical engineer. He concludes his report as follows:

"I own, I never till lately gave much attention to the business or art of fortifying harbors or building forts, batteries, etc, but the alarming situation and distress in which our country is in, and ministerial designs and vengeance aimed at our seacoast, have called my attention to look into matters of that kind; and so far as I can judge, it is of the utmost importance to secure the port and harbor of New London from falling into the hands of our enemies, which will be an asylum for ships, vessels of force, floating batteries, etc., that may be, by the continent or any particular government, built for the protection of our seacoast trade or country, which shall come that way; but on the contrary, if left destitute of protection and fall into the hands of our enemies, it would let them into the bowels of our country and give them great advantage against us; that the best and only sure and eligible manner of fortifying and securing said port and harbor is, in erecting batteries at the several places and in some manner as before mentioned."

On the 9th of January, 1776, Colonel Elderkin was appointed to go to Salisbury and procure the casting of cannon for the State, and on the 29th he made a report on the subject. February 2d, of the same year, he was directed to go again to Salisbury and have cannon balls cast at Smith's furnace. During most of the year 1776 he was actively employed by the State, in executing various commissions, such as procuring ordnance, purchasing supplies, taking charge of prisoners, etc., besides driving the powder mills at Willimantic, about which more will be said hereafter. He was sent to Boston to inquire for the best model for cannon of 18 pounds, or less. In May, 1777, he was directed to procure six men and twelve horses and go to Portsmouth, N. H., and apply to John Langdon, Esq., for six brass field pieces and bring them to this State. The above are only samples of the commissions that he was frequently called upon to execute. If anything was to be done requiring business energy and promptness, Colonel Elderkin was the man selected. When it is recollected that he was at this time a lawyer of extensive practice, and a portion of the time State's attorney for Windham county, that he was a member of the General Assembly, one of the Governor's Council of Safety, that he was a large land-holder, and at the same time a manufacturer, it will readily be admitted that he was a man of ability, great activity and executive talent. We have seen that Col. Elderkin was active in the service of the State in various capacities, such as procuring ordnance and supplies for the army, and executing different commissions in the early part of the Revolutionary war. The need of powder was as great as for ordnance and small arms, and there was at the commencement of the war no powder manufactory in the State. Col. Elderkin, in company with Nathaniel Wales, Jr., made a successful effort to supply this great want. Mr. Wales, like Col. Elderkin, was an ardent patriot, a local Judge, a member of the Governor's Council of Safety, and a talented and influential citizen of Windham. He was very active in town affairs, and generally presided at important meetings held during the revolution. At a special session of the Legislature, in December, 1775, it was enacted, "That a bounty or premium of £30 should be paid out of the treasury to the person who should erect the *first powder mill* in the colony and manufacture five hundred pounds of good merchantable gunpowder" The same premium was offered in regard to the second mill.

It was enacted that no powder mill should be erected in the colony without a license from the General Assembly under a penalty of £30. At the same session (December, 1775,) liberty was given to Jedediah Elderkin and Nathaniel Wales, Jr, to erect a powder mill in Windham pursuant to the act of Assembly. The place chosen for the site of their mill was at Willimantic, then a cluster of some half dozen houses with a grist and saw mill. The eastern portion of the Linen Company's thread mill now occupies its site. The work of erecting the mill was pushed with vigor and completed early in the spring of 1776. At the May session of the Legislature, 1776, Elderkin & Wales were allowed £30 premium "for one thousand pounds of powder previously manufactured by them." Theirs was probably the first powder mill erected in the State, though Colonel Pitkin, of East Hartford, built one about the same time. On April 29th, 1776, permit was given to Adam Babcock, of New Haven, to purchase of Elderkin & Wales 200 pounds of powder for his privateer, then fitting out. The earliest order found on Col. Pitkin for powder was June 28th, 1776. Governor Trumbull, in a letter to Congress, states that the Willimantic and Hartford powder mills were both in full operation previous to June 4th, 1776, and that another one was nearly completed. The Willimantic mill continued to furnish large quantities of powder until December 13, 1777, when it blew up, killing Boswell Moulton, one of the workmen, a young man aged about 22 years. The works were pretty thoroughly destroyed and the mill was never rebuilt so far as is known. The powder made here greatly aided the colonies in their struggle, and the New London paper in announcing the destruction of the works, December 19, says: "Amongst other obstacles to impede our success, last Friday, the powder mill at Windham blew up." The difficulties in the way of starting a new manufactory of the kind, at such short notice—of procuring machinery, material and skilled workmen—was very great indeed, and that they were so successfully overcome in such a short period of time we think is due in a great measure to the enterprise and energy of Col. Elderkin." The purchase of the site for the powder mill included the grain and saw mill near by, which were owned by Colonel Elderkin at his death.

Colonel Elderkin is deserving honorable mention for his experiments in the manufacture of silk. It is a matter of regret that so little is known in regard to his efforts and success in this, then untried, branch of industry. But that he made a determined effort in this direction at an early day and achieved a measure of success is certain. It seems that in the early part of the Seventeenth century the English government, having failed in their experiments with the silk worm at home, were very desirous of introducing it into the provinces of Georgia and Carolina, and in order to induce the colonists to engage in the business all duties were removed, and soon after a bounty was offered on all raw silk imported from the colonies. This led to the formation of a company in Philadelphia, of which Dr. Franklin was the agent in England. The date of the formation of this association is unknown, as well as its influence in extending the manufacture of silk. The venerable Zalmon Storrs, Esq., in a note to Wm. L. Weaver, dated the 18th day of December, 1864, says: "I think the production of silk was commenced in this town (Mansfield Center) the first of any place in Connecticut. The seed of the mulberry and the eggs of the worm came from Long Island. Silk was produced here many years before the Revolutionary war. Nathaniel Aspenwall, of this town, became quite an enthusiast on the subject, planted a large nursery in New Haven and other places; and I remember hearing him say that he took two silk vest patterns to Philadelphia while Congress was in session there and made a present of one to General Washington and the other to Dr. Franklin." A descendant of Col. Elderkin thinks he was the first to introduce the silk worm into Connecticut, but we are inclined to believe Mr. Storrs is correct, and that it was first introduced into Mansfield Center. It is quite probable, however, that Col. Elderkin began about the same time, as he had his weaving done at Mansfield, and it may be he was connected with that company. At any rate he was one of the pioneers in this important branch of industry, and deserves great credit for his enterprise and zeal in the business. The following is a letter written by Col. Elderkin to Clement Biddle, Esq., of Philadelphia, a member of the association above referred to:

WINDHAM, January 22, 1773.

SIR—I am informed that you are one of those gentlemen in your Province who are confederated together to carry on the silk manufactory, and have made great proficiency therein, in prosecution of which I wish you success.

In the meantime would inform you that some years since I began the cultivation of the mulberry tree, having now a large number fit for improvement. Two years past have made considerable quantities of silk ; have spun and improved some, but find in that part of the process in spinning from the ball we fail, for want of proper reels and experienced workmen ; have been seeking and looking out for help herein. For that purpose got Eb. Gray, when at Philadelphia, last fall, to inquire, and by whom I am informed of your undertaking and proceeding in the laudable branch of making silk, and that one of the young women in your works would be prevailed on to come here for a year, and that reels might be had or were made with you of the right kind, with all the apparatus for the spinning of silk from the ball ; on which information I determined early in the spring to send my son to you to procure a hand and a reel and bring home with him. I desire therefore that you would get me a reel with all its appurtenances and cauldron made as soon as may be, and also to assist me in procuring the woman to whom Mr. Gray made some proposals in my behalf, to come. When I send my son shall send the money for the reel ; he will wait upon and assist the woman in getting here. Your assistance in the above matters will help in promoting the purpose of making silk in North America, and greatly oblige your unknown Friend and Obed't and hum'l Serv't,

JEDEDIAH ELDERKIN.

P. S.—Please on the receipt of this send me a line per post, to be left at N. London, and charge the postage of letter."

The mulberry orchard of Col. Elderkin was on what is called the Wanton Perry farm, near the village of South Windham. In his will, dated March 15th, 1792, Col. Elderkin speaks of his "mulberry lands near Auwebetuck," and "the appurtenances belonging to my silk manufactory." It seems by this that he had a silk factory, and there are those living now (1865) who remember seeing the fabric made at his establishment.

The daughters of Col. Elderkin, it is said, had handkerchiefs and dresses made from the silk he manufactured. It seems from the date of his letter to Philadelphia and the date of his will that he was engaged in the manufacture of silk over twenty-one years after his mulberry trees were large enough to improve by the use of the worm. He must have made the business profitable or he would not have pursued it for so great a length of time. It is said that Col. Elderkin imported a weaver from England.

He continued in the practice of his profession, which was extensive, until age and ill-health compelled him to abandon it. His last, and, in some respects, most important public service was as member of the convention in this State which ratified the United States Constitution. It was quite appropriate that he, who had labored so earnestly and faithfully to secure the independence of his country, should be permitted, as the crowning act of his life, to vote for a constitution which secured the blessings of liberty and free government to his posterity. As so few living remember Colonel Elderkin we obtain our impressions of his talents and character mainly from his public life. Judging from that we feel assured that he was an ardent and devoted patriot. He not only fully sympathized with the people of his town, but he was one of their most honored and trusted leaders from the beginning to the close of the revolutionary struggle. He was confided in and honored by Governor Trumbull and the General Assembly during the war as few men were; and for the important services rendered the country in its hour of greatest need and peril his name should ever be held in grateful remembrance. He had practical business talents. He was active, prompt and persevering. He was a man for an emergency. He was capable of originating new enterprises and carrying them out under the greatest difficulties and discouragements. He knew no such word as fail, and had nothing of the old fogy about him. His character for probity and integrity was, so far as we can learn, without a stain.

Colonel Elderkin was quite successful in accumulating property, yet we judge he was a benevolent and liberal-minded man. He spent his money freely for the benefit of his family, and we presume for worthy public and private purposes. He educated two of his sons at Yale College and prepared the other to enter.

He is remembered by a few aged persons as a large, tall and very fine-looking man, with the manners of an English gentleman.

The following obituary notice of him is copied from the Windham *Herald* under the head of deaths, dated March 9, 1793:

"In this town on the 3d inst., after a long and painful illness, endured with singular patience, departed this life JEDEDIAH ELDERKIN, Esq., in the 75th year of his age, who for many years was an eminent and honorable practitioner of law in this State, and by much improvement in several important stations in life, was, for many years, a very useful member of society. In his death the surviving partner laments the loss of a tender husband; a numerous offspring, that of a kind and affectionate parent, and the needy sufferer, the loss of a benevolent and charitable friend."

The will of Colonel Elderkin is dated March 15, 1792, and proved March 27, 1793. In it he says *he has disposed of most of his property by deeds of gift to his children.* To his wife Anne he gives the use and improvement of his grist and saw mill during her life, with a horse, carriage, cow and household goods. Also of the house and lands where his son Bela now lives, near the mills, his mulberry lands near Auwebetuck, with buildings, etc., on that farm, with all the appurtenances belonging to his silk manufactory, in fee simple. Said mulberry lands and trees being reserved in his deed of said farm to David Young. He gives to his grandson Jedediah, son of his son Bela, two-thirds part of estate in grist mill, equal to one-fourth part of the whole in fee simple, directing him to render to his father all profits of his said share in said mills immediately after the decease of his grandmother and during the life of his father, if he lives and stands in need of such supply. To his son Vine he gives his French gun, sword and ornaments of dress, (his gold and silver cuff buttons, knee and shoe buckles, are now, 1886, in the hands of Henry Elderkin, son of Dr. Vine Elderkin, who resides near Ashville, Chautauqua county, N. Y.), and to Bela his other gun and fowling piece. He gives to Alfred his share in the Proprietor's School lot and house. To Sophia Flint, daughter of his daughter Lora, deceased, he gives £20. His wife was named executrix, but probably on account of age and infirmity she declined to act, and his son Alfred was appointed in her stead. Colonel Jedediah Elderkin married Anna Wood, who is remembered by some as an excellent woman and worthy companion of her honored husband. Unlike him she was small size. She was four years younger than he, and survived him eleven years. They had eight children.

Colonel Jedediah Elderkin was born 1717.

Anne Wood was born 1721.

They were married August 31st, 1741.

He died March 3 (in his 75th year), 1793.

She died June 14 (aged 83 years), 1804.

FIFTH GENERATION—THEIR CHILDREN.

NAMES.	BORN.	MARRIED TO.	DATE OF MAR.	DIED.
1 Judith.	March 2, 1743.	Hon. J. Huntington.	Aug. 6, 1760.	Sept. 24, 1786.
2 Vine.	Sept. 11, 1746.	Lydia White.	Nov. 23, 1767.	Aug. 5, 1800.
3 Annie.	Oct. 30, 1747.	Hezekiah Bissell.	March 18, 1765.	
4 Bela.	Dec. 10, 1751.	Philena Fitch.	March 18, 1773.	
5 Lora.	Nov. 30. 1753.	Royal Flint.		1791.
6 Alfred.	Jan. 4, 1759.	Sarah Brown.	Jan. 27, 1779.	Oct. 9, 1833.
7 Amie.	March 6, 1761.	Jabez Clark.	April 4, 1787.	July 2d, 1838.
8 Charlotte.	Oct. 23, 1764.	Samuel Gray.	July 2, 1788.	Dec. 13, 1797.
Nameless son.	April 24. 1756.			May 1, 1756.

CHAPTER III.

Dr. Joshua Elderkin, a younger brother of Colonel Jedediah Elderkin, was born at Norwich October 30, 1720. He graduated at Yale College in 1748, studied theology and was ordained pastor of the Society of Old Haddam June, 1749. He remained there only a few years, when, from poor health and other reasons, he was dismissed in 1753. Afterwards he studied medicine, it is thought with Dr. Jonathan Huntington, then a prominent practitioner in Windham. That he practiced medicine in that town several years we are assured by his descendants. But it appears he had ability to turn his hand to more than one kind of business. Some time before the Revolutionary war he was engaged in trade, and while in mercantile business he sold some articles of foreign manufacture, contrary to a resolution of the town not to import, sell or use in their families those foreign made articles. For this act he remained for about four years under a very severe censure from the people of his town. Though Dr. Elderkin was a man of strong will power and firmness he did not rest quite easy under this censure. The matter was finally disposed of at a town meeting, December 9, 1774. We are unable to say how culpable Dr. Elderkin was in the matter of selling the hats and vest patterns, but the manner in which he was treated at the outset undoubtedly roused his feelings, and it was a good while before he would make any explanations or take any steps towards a reconciliation.

But as matters between the colonies and mother country became more serious and the danger of collision imminent, feelings of discord were banished and all true patriots felt the necessity of acting harmoniously. Dr. Elderkin's services were needed. He was an educated man of business experience and energy. The difficulty was happily settled, and from that time Dr. Elderkin fully shared the confidence of his fellow citizens. He was, like his brother, ardently patriotic, and rendered most important services during the most trying period of the revolutionary war. In July, 1776, he was appointed to buy tow cloth for tents for the army. In the same year he was appointed with others to procure supplies and refreshments for the soldiers. At one time an order of £1,000 was drawn in his favor for the purchase of clothing. His name is often mentioned in the doings of the Assembly and Council of Safety as furnishing supplies and providing and contracting for various articles necessary for the army. One descendant says: He entered heart and soul into the war of the revolution, was early commissary in the army, and to help forward the cause pledged his fortune for debts contracted in its service. Government paid in Continental money, which, at the close of the war, greatly depreciating in value, his own property was taken to pay these debts, and, that not being sufficient, he was thrown into Windham jail, where he spent many months. He and his wife in their last days found a home with their youngest daughter in Canterbury (Westminster Society), where they died and were buried in the cemetery of that place. He was truly in every sense a good man. His career was a checkered one, and he experienced many ups and downs in life. His services and sacrifiçes for his country in its most trying period should lead us to pardon his versatile organization and with gratitude remember his virtues.

Dr. Joshua Elderkin was born October 30, 1720.

He married Rachel Wetmore July 31, 1749.

He died (aged 80 years) at Windham, February, 1801.

Neither the birth nor death of his wife is known.

Besides two who died in infancy they had:

FIFTH GENERATION—THE FOLLOWING CHILDREN.

NAMES.	BORN.	MARRIED TO.	DATE OF MAR.	DIED.
1 Hannah.	April 24, 1750.			Aug. 17, 1750
2 Joshua Booth	June 14, 1751.	Lydia Denison.	Oct. 16, 1769.	
3 Lo'saRachel.	May 31, 1753.	Samuel Badger.	(No heirs).	
4 Susannah.	Nov. 7, 1760.	Roger Huntington.		
5 Hannah II.	Feb. 26, 1764.	Samuel Johnson.	(of Canterb'ry)	
		2 Alexand'r Gordon	"	
		3 Joshua Grosvenor	(of Pomfret).	

Joshua Booth Elderkin was born June 14, 1751.

It was said by a cousin of his that he was a very large and strong man, possessing powers rarely equaled. He lived down town while he remained in Windham, and built the brick house which stands where the road turns toward the burying ground. It is said he kept hotel there during the Revolution, and that the French officers boarded with him so late as 1780. At what time he left Windham is not known. One account says he went to Chelsea, Vt., where he died. Another that he went to Middlebury, Vt.

Joshua Booth Elderkin married Lydia Denison October 16, 1769.

SIXTH GENERATION—THEIR CHILDREN.

NAMES.	BORN.	MARRIED TO.	DATE OF MAR.	DIED.
1 Mary.	July 16, 1770.	Daniel Perkins.	Lived in Chel	sea, Vt.
2 Lydia.	Oct. 17. 1773.	Jabez Fitch, of	Willimantic a	nd Lebanon
		2 Azariah Balcam,	of Mansfield &	Willimantic.
3 Rachel Ann.	Oct. 13, 1774.			
4 Sarah Wales,	Feb. 25, 1776.			
5 JoshuaBooth	Jan. 3, 1779.	Married and lived	at Middlebury	
6 Louisa R.	Feb. 13, 1781.			
7 Alathea.	May 30, 1784.	Jairus Littlefield,	Lived at Willi	mantic
8 Nancy.	It is said marrie	d Shurtliff, lived in	Montreal.	
9 Lucretia.		Phelps, lived in New	York.	
10 Luceus. }	Were twins. No	Lived in Middlebur	y, Vt.	
11 Lucia. }	acc't of Lucia.			

Lydia Elderkin, daughter of Joshua Booth Elderkin, married, 1st, Jabez Fitch, who lived in Willimantic and Lebanon. She was the mother of

SEVENTH GENERATION.

Eleazer D. Fitch, of Willimantic.

Mrs. Laban Chase, of Willimantic.

Col. E. S. Fitch, of Mansfield.

She married, 2d, Azariah Balcam, of Mansfield, who afterwards lived in Willimantic, where they both died.

Alathea Elderkin married Jairus Littlefield ; had a family in Willimantic, where she lived and died.

Susannah Elderkin, fourth child of Dr. Joshua Elderkin, married Roger Huntington, of Windham.

SIXTH GENERATION—THEIR CHILDREN.

1 Hulda, who married Anson Johnson, of Plainfield.

2 Eunice, who married George Wyllys Abbe, of Windham.

3 Betsey, who married Murray Johnson, of Plainfield.

4 Harry, who married Clarissa Bibbins ; had family ; died in Windham.

5 Joshua, who lived in Windham ; died unmarried.

Hannah Huntington Elderkin, fifth child of Dr. Joshua Elderkin, married Samuel Johnson, of Canterbury ; had one child, Salome, who married Artemus Osgood, of Pomfret. Hannah H. Johnson married, 2d, Alexander Gordon, of Canterbury, and by him had two children, Maria, who died unmarried, and Harriet, who married Deacon Charles Lee, of Willimantic, who died at Norwich, leaving Harriet a widow. Mrs. Hannah H. Gordon married, 3d, Deacon Joshua Grosvenor, of Pomfret (Abington Society), where she died July 8th, 1834. Her children were the Sixth Generation.

FOURTH GENERATION.—John Elderkin 4th, brother of Col. Jedediah E., was born February, 1719. Married Rebecca Allen, daughter of Timothy Allen, March 2, 1742.

FIFTH GENERATION—THEIR CHILDREN.

NAMES.	BORN.	MARRIED TO.	DATE OF MAR.	DIED.
1 John 5th,	Jan. 18, 1742.	(Graduated at Yale	College.	
2 Susannah.	Oct. 7, 1745.	Eleazer Denison.	(Had a large family).	
3 Luther.	Sept. 6, 1746.			
4 Rebecca.	Sept. 17, 1748.			
5 Joshua.	Jan. 13, 1750.			
6 Judges.	Aug. 23, 1752.			Aug., 1753.
7 Vashti.	July 19, 1754.	Elias Bingham, of Scotland.		
8 Francis.	Feb. 11, 1757.			May 21, 1759.
9 Raxaleny.	Sept. 5, 1759.			
10 Dyarchey.	April 7, 1762.			
11 Fernando.	July 9, 1764			

CHAPTER IV.

At this point of our work we will suspend the further exhibit of the Elderkin families for a space to introduce the Dyer and White families, who, as cotemporaries with Col. Jedediah Elderkin, became, by marriage, identified with the descendants of one child of Col. Jedediah, viz, Vine, his oldest son.

RECORD OF THE DYER FAMILY.—BY HANNAH CLARK.

THIRD GENERATION—Captain Thomas Dyer was born May 15, 1694. Lydia Backus, his wife, was born June 15, 1695.

FOURTH GENERATION—THEIR CHILDREN.

1. Mary Dyer, born January 31, 1719; Died May 27, 1802. She married Rev. Stephen White, of Upper Middleton, Conn. They had ten children.

2. Col. Eliphalet Dyer, born September 14, 1721. He was an eminent lawyer of Windham, Conn., and the intimate friend and companion of Col. Jedediah Elderkin.

3. Lydia Dyer, born July 12, 1724.

4. Eunice Dyer, born June 5, 1727.

FOURTH GENERATION—Rev. Stephen White was born in Upper Middleton, Conn., June 8, 1718. He was a descendant of Elder John White, one of the founders of Hartford, Conn. He is the fifth generation, counting Elder John, but is really the cotemporary of the fourth generation of the Elderkin family. He graduated at Yale College in 1736, was ordained pastor of the Congregational Church in Windham, Conn., December 24, 1740. He ministered to the same church over fifty-three years. He married Mary Dyer September 2, 1741. They had ten children. He died January 9, 1794, aged 76. She died May 27, 1802, aged 83.

FIFTH GENERATION—THEIR CHILDREN.

NAMES.	BORN.	MARRIED TO.	DATE OF MAR.	DIED.
1 Hannah.	Dec. 20, 1742.			
2 Mary.	Dec. 23, 1743.			
3 Lydia.	April 28, 1745.	Vine Elderkin.		
4 Susannah.	Oct. 21, 1746.			
5 Eunice.	Jan. 7, 1749.			
6 John.	Oct. 3, 1752.	Edu'd at Yale Coll.		
7 Elisha.	Sept. 16, 1754.	Miss Webb, of Windham.		
8 Sarah.	Nov. 10, 1757.			
9 Hulda.	April 11, 1760.			
10 Dyer.	May 20, 1762.	Edu'd at Yale Coll.		

Elisha White had three children. Myra married Mr. Chamberlain; lives in Michigan.

For the purpose of presenting one line of the White family in a condensed diagram I extract from the March number of the "Laws of Life," a family health journal, conducted by the Faculty of our "Home on the Hillside," The Sanitarium, Dansville, N. Y., an article entitled "The Economics of Marriage; a Family Record, by Phineas Wood."

There have recently come into my hands certain faded and antique looking papers, containing a page of family history, which on several accounts I think may be interesting to the readers of this journal. Aside from their personal character, the facts are valuable in other respects. It is partly the history of a pilgrim and a pioneer, who came to New England in the early days of its history, and partly the record of a single branch of his family, from generation to generation—down through more than two centuries and a half, to the present day.

On the 23d of June, 1632, only twelve years from the first

landing of the pilgrims, a little bark with 123 passengers, of whom fifty were children, set sail from the coast of England for the New World. After a twelve weeks' voyage—spending, as it were, an entire summer in mid-ocean—the tired travelers landed at the newly-founded settlement of Boston, September 16th of the same year. Among them was Elder John White, a leading member of the congregation of the Rev. Thomas Hooker, which, for the most part, comprised the passengers of the vessel. Mr. Hooker himself was prevented from accompanying his flock, but came over to the colony the following year.

In the town of Cambridge, adjoining Boston, John White made his first home in America. The beautiful library building of Harvard University, "Gore Hall," stands to-day upon a portion of his home lot.

For several reasons, however, the atmosphere of Massachusetts Bay was not quite pleasant to Mr. Hooker and his people, and they determined, therefore, to found a new settlement where greater freedom might be enjoyed than probably existed then in that latitude. In June, 1636, the main body of his congregation, among them John White, started through the trackless wilderness for their new home in the valley of the Connecticut. With no guide but their compass, they made their way through swamps, over mountains and across rivers, driving before them their herds of cattle; and after a fortnight's hardships reached their destination, and laid the foundations of Hartford, the capital of Connecticut. Here, under the very shadow of a tree, destined later on to be famous in colonial history, the "Charter Oak," John White for a second time established his home in the New World.

He was not destined even here to pass undisturbed the remainder of his days. Hartford treated him with honor; he was one of her original proprietors, and four times he was chosen as one of her "Selectmen," who had in charge the interests of the settlement. But after the death of Mr.

Hooker dissentions arose in the church. Perhaps there was a good deal of "the old Adam" in our pilgrim ancestors; a pugnacity that resisted opposition and grew restive for independence under the least semblance of restraint; but that is the class of men to found cities and establish empires. A large portion of Mr. Hooker's congregation concluded to make a new settlement far up the Connecticut at the town of Hadley, and White was a leading spirit in the enterprise. But although Hadley chose him as her representative to the Legislative Assembly in Boston, he seems to have had a lingering love for Hartford, and to have returned thither in his old age; and here in the winter of 1684, just two hundred years ago, the old puritan-pioneer rested from his labors at the age of 75 years.

I shall not attempt to sketch in detail the biography of his descendants, but rather to present in a diagram those facts about a particular line of descent as shall answer my purpose. There were large families born to each descendant of John White, but now we have to do with but a single child of each generation down to the present time. If the reader will note that the connecting lines between the names run from parent to child he will have no difficulty in tracing downward the line of descent.

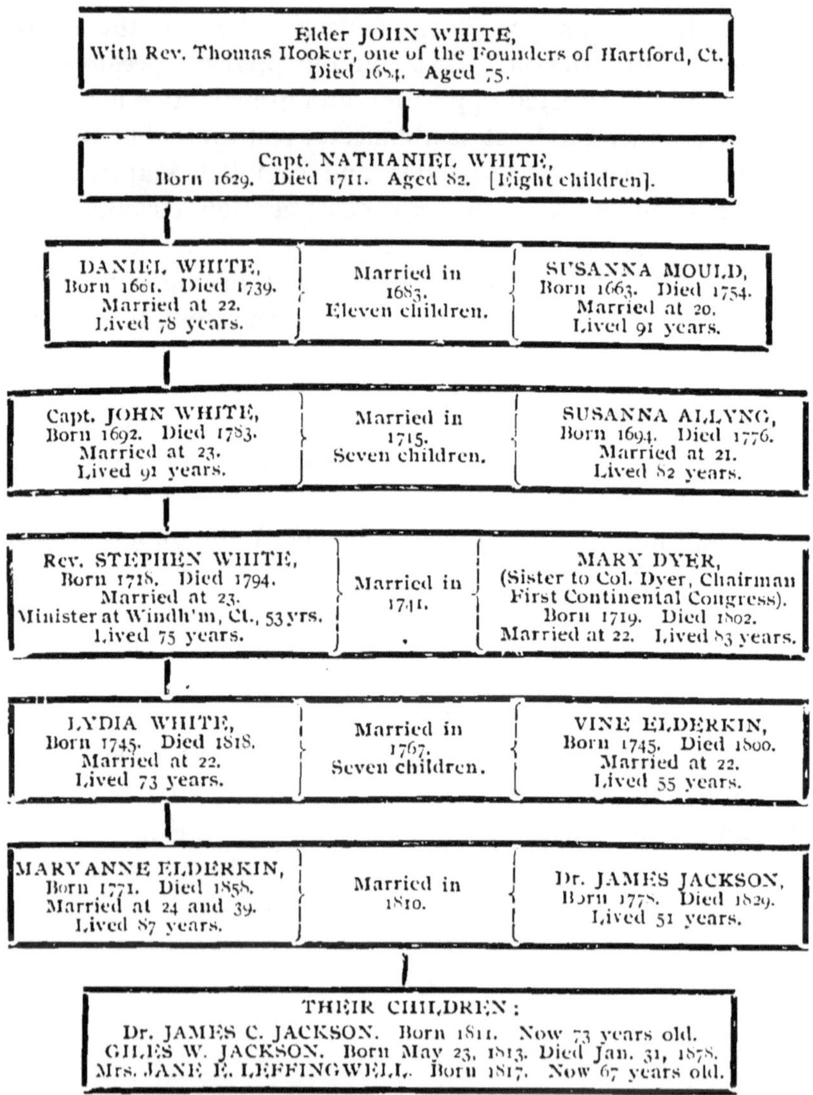

Elder JOHN WHITE,
With Rev. Thomas Hooker, one of the Founders of Hartford, Ct.
Died 1684. Aged 75.
Capt. NATHANIEL WHITE,
Born 1629. Died 1711. Aged 82. [Eight children].
DANIEL WHITE,
Born 1661. Died 1739.
Married at 22.
Lived 78 years.
Married in 1683.
Eleven children.
SUSANNA MOULD,
Born 1663. Died 1754.
Married at 20.
Lived 91 years.
Capt. JOHN WHITE,
Born 1692. Died 1783.
Married at 23.
Lived 91 years.
Married in 1715.
Seven children.
SUSANNA ALLYNG,
Born 1694. Died 1776.
Married at 21.
Lived 82 years.
Rev. STEPHEN WHITE,
Born 1718. Died 1794.
Married at 23.
Minister at Windh'm, Ct., 53 yrs.
Lived 75 years.
Married in 1741.
MARY DYER,
(Sister to Col. Dyer, Chairman First Continental Congress).
Born 1719. Died 1802.
Married at 22. Lived 83 years.
LYDIA WHITE,
Born 1745. Died 1818.
Married at 22.
Lived 73 years.
Married in 1767.
Seven children.
VINE ELDERKIN,
Born 1745. Died 1800.
Married at 22.
Lived 55 years.
MARY ANNE ELDERKIN,
Born 1771. Died 1858.
Married at 24 and 39.
Lived 87 years.
Married in 1810.
Dr. JAMES JACKSON,
Born 1778. Died 1829.
Lived 51 years.
THEIR CHILDREN:
Dr. JAMES C. JACKSON. Born 1811. Now 73 years old.
GILES W. JACKSON. Born May 23, 1813. Died Jan. 31, 1878.
Mrs. JANE E. LEFFINGWELL. Born 1817. Now 67 years old.

How brief are these records of the past! Here, on little oblong diagrams we trace the simple outline of many a long life. Experience that was crowded into seventy, eighty, even ninety years, leaves behind for posterity the dates of a birth, a marriage—and a death. It is so little! And yet is it not the epitome of most earthly existence? Two hundred years hence, shall a far posterity, looking backward from the twenty-first century, care to remember our lives of to-day so kindly, so gratefully, and so reverently as these memories are held?

What may we learn from this record?

I. That on one side, at least, of each generation, *long life was hereditary.* Five generations of mothers and grandmothers, in direct descent, attain respectively the ages of 87, 73, 83, 82 and 91 years, an average of 83 1-5 years. I do not know of a similar instance on record. Seven generations of fathers and grandfathers average 72½ years. Even this is beyond the allotted time.

II. As a rule, the wives lived longer than their husbands. This is the case in four out of five instances in which ages are known.

III. *They married early*, disregarding all those wise maxims of prudential philosophy so current in the theory and practice of our time. Each of these grandmothers married between 20 and 24, at an average somewhat less than 22 years, while the average age of their husbands was just under 24 years. The one who married youngest attained the greatest age; the one who married latest was the shortest lived.

IV. They rejoiced in large families of children. The details in this respect of all the families are not in my possession; but of those known, the average is eight children to each couple. Golden weddings were almost hereditary, three successive generations living far beyond the fiftieth anniversary of their marriage day.

V. I do not believe that any of them were rich as wealth is reckoned to-day. One was a country clergyman, ministering over fifty-three years to a single congregation; one was a sea captain, and the others were farmers and artisans, in comfortable circumstances, but not superabundant wealth.

Nearly every young man expected to leave his parents and make a fortune for himself. Only one of the seven died in the place of his birth. When beyond her eightieth year one of these venerable women wrote with trembling hand a little record of her early life Here are some extracts :

"February 3d, 17—, being then in my twenty-fourth year, I was married. We were both poor, but had good health and good habits. My husband came of an excellent family ; his great-grandfather was Rev. Jonathan Edwards, the divine. We determined to make ourselves a home in 'the western country,' as Central New York was then called ; and accordingly, the week after marriage, started on our journey. * * The roads through the wilderness were almost impassable ; we were obliged to go on horseback, finding our path by marked trees.

My husband had purchased 130 acres of land, and here he cleared a spot sufficient to erect a small log house The floor was of hewn logs. The first work my husband did was to cut down the trees near our house, after which he began to clear land for the fall crops. Whenever he was alone in the woods, at the falling of each tree, I listened till I heard the sound of his ax again, which told me no accident had befallen him. The howling of the wolves at night disturbed me a great deal at first.

Some of my Connecticut friends, writing to me, asked how we managed with the *one chair* we had brought from home. I replied that 'when my husband needed it I sat in his lap.' My first baby was born the following November. We attended meeting in Butler's barn, riding on horseback —my husband carrying the baby and I riding behind him. * * Eight years we lived here ; four other children were born to us, and in one sense these were the happiest years of my life.

Can we wonder at it? Why, this rude cabin, with its rough hewn floor and its single chair—these innocent, loving hearts, this young wife whispering her first secret to her youthful husband one happy evening during that long, expectant summer, suggest a vision of happiness so celestial, that I do not wonder it stirred her memory to its depths when her cheek was withered and her eye was dim, and the events of yesterday were a forgotten blank. Oh, calculating theorist, do not dream that those oft-repeated maxims of a selfish prudence have taught you the secret of a happier life

CHAPTER V.

We will here present the family records so far as known of Col. Jedediah Elderkin's daughters.

Judith married Hon. Jabez Huntington, a lawyer and High Sheriff of Windham County. They had nine children. Nancy married Guerdon Bachus, a slave-owner in Virginia. Annie married Dea. Hezekiah Bissel, a lawyer and State's Attorney for Windham county. They had eight children. The oldest son, Woodbridge, was educated at Yale College. Amelia married Rev. Abel Flint, of Hartford, and had one daughter, the wife of Rev. Herman Norton, Secretary of the American Protestant Society.

Lora married Royal Flint (brother of Rev. Abel Flint), a merchant near West Point, and owner of a large tract of land. He lost his property by signing notes as surety. Then moved South, where he died, leaving one daughter, Sophia, who married Erastus Clark, of Utica, N. Y. Lora lost an infant son, born April 24th, 1756; died May 1st, 1756.

Amie married Jabez Clark, a lawyer of Windham, Conn., April 4, 1787. Died at Utica, N. Y., July 2, 1838.

THEIR CHILDREN—SIXTH GENERATION.

NAMES.	BORN.	MARRIED TO.	DATE OF MAR.	DIED.
1 Charles.	1788			1798.
2 Elizabeth.	Oct., 1789.	Walter King.	(Of Utica).	1812.
3 Anna.	1792.	Edward Vernon.		
4 Jerusia.	Mar., 1794.	Jessee W. Doolittle.		Oct., 1865.
5 Edward.	Feb., 1796.	Harriet Perkins.		Mar., 1868.
6 Charlotte E.	Oct., 1798.	Sam'l Perkins.	(Of Phila.)	Jan., 1823.
7 Edwards.		Hannah Perkins.	(Of Windham)	

Charlotte married Samuel Gray, Esq., educated at Yale College. She died, aged 33, leaving three children. Harriet married Oliver C Grosvenor, of Pomfret. Mary, widow of Samuel Byrne, married Thomas Gray, Esq., many years Town Clerk of Windham.

CHAPTER VI.

In following the descent of Col. Jedediah Elderkin's three sons, Vine, Bela and Alfred, we will first trace Vine's descendants in their order down to the present date—1884. Then Bela's, then Alfred's, so far as we may be able to find their records.

FIFTH GENERATION.—Capt. Vine Elderkin, Esq., was born in Windham, Conn., Sept. 11, 1745. Lydia White, daughter of Rev. Stephen White, was born in Windham, April 28, 1745.

They were married Nov. 23, 1767.

He died in Albany at the residence of his daughter, Julianna Staniford, with dropsy, Aug. 15, 1800. Lydia died Oct. 2, 1818, at Windham, Conn.

Capt. Vine graduated at Yale College at the age of 18 years, and was engaged in the mercantile business in New York City at the time of the breaking out of the Revolution, when he entered the army as Captain, where he endured the hardships and deprivations attending that terrible struggle for American Independence. He was an excellent man, a firm adherent to all the principles of integrity and morality; too generous to become affluent, and too humane to seek popularity and position at the expense of his compeers. His wife was a noble woman; educated and refined, patriotic and industrious. She supported their family during her husband's absence by book-keeping in New York.

The preceding description of Capt. Vine Elderkin, Esq., is reported by Mary Anne Roberts, from the records of Hannah (Clark) Roberts, as she heard it from her mother, Mary Anne (Elderkin) Clark. The following is as published in the Willimantic *Journal* by William L. Weaver: "Vine Elderkin, eldest son of Col. Jedediah, was born in Windham. * * * He studied law, probably with his father, and having been admitted to practice, settled in Windham, where he attained considerable eminence as an advocate and councellor. Subsequently he removed to the State of New York, and, as we are informed, settled on the Hudson, somewhere near West Point, where he had charge of an iron foundry." I judge that grandfather Vine practiced the doctrine of non-resistance in too liberal a sense. It will do in moral and religious practice, but in the conflicts of a business life the Jewish law, "An eye for an eye and a tooth for a tooth," is much more practical.

THEIR CHILDREN—SIXTH GENERATION.

NAMES.	BORN.	MARRIED TO.	DATE OF MAR.	DIED.
1 Harriet.	Oct. 4, 1768.	James Jackson.		Sept., 1809.
2 Bela.	Feb. 3, 1770.	Susan Bates.	1796.	Aug. 3, 1853.
3 Mary Anne.	Dec. 18, 1771.	Henry Clark.	1795	July 19, 1858.
	1778.	Dr. James Jackson.	1810.	1829.
4 Step'n White	Sept. 12, 1773.	Mary Powell, wid'w.		1856.
5 Julianna,	Jan. 20, 1776.	Timothy Staniford.	Nov. 14, 1775.	Oct. 27, 1844.
6 Lucy.	Nov. 27, 1778.	Joseph Strong.		1819.
7 Charlotte.	Mar. 23, 1781.	Charles Moseley.		1866

It is said that the marriages of this family, with one exception, were more than ordinarily good.

Harriet Elderkin married Dr. James Jackson, of Manlius, N. Y. She died, leaving one daughter, Harriet Jackson, who married Cromlin Brown, and died leaving no child.

This little poem, by Mrs. Julia C. R. Doir, was written from a well authenticated incident in the life of Harriet Elderkin, who, at the time of the occurrence, was living with her grandfather, Parson White:

THE PARSON'S GRANDDAUGHTER.

"Ho ho!" he cried, as up and down
He rode through the streets of Windham town.

"Ho! ho! for the day of peace is done,
And the day of wrath too well begun!
Bring forth your grain from your barns and mills;
Drive down the cattle from off your hills;
For Boston lieth in sore distress,
Pallid with hunger and long duress,
Her children starve while she hears the beat
And the tramp of the redcoats on every street!"

What, ho! What, ho! Like a storm unspent,
Over the hillsides he came and went;
And Parson White, from his open door,
Leaning bare-headed that August day,
While the sun beat down on his temples gray,
Watched him until he could see no more.
Then straight he strode to the church and flung
His whole soul into the peal, he rung;
Pulling the bell-rope till the tower
Seemed to rock in the sudden shower.
The shower of sound the farmers heard,
Rending the air like a living word!

Then swift they gathered, with right good will,
From field and anvil and shop and mill,
To hear what the parson had to say
That would not keep till the Sabbath day.
For only the women and children knew
The tale of the horseman galloping through—
The message he bore, as up and down
He rode through the streets of Windham town.
That night, as the parson sat at ease
In the porch, with the Bible on his knees,
Thanking God that at break of day
Frederic Manning would take his way,
With cattle and sheep from off the hills,
And a load of grain from the barns and mills
To the starving city, where General Gage
Waited unholy war to wage.

His little daughter beside him stood,
Hiding her face in her muslin hood.
In her arms her own pet lamb she bore,
As it struggled down to the oaken floor:

"It must go; I must give my lamb," she said,
"To the children that cry for meat and bread."
Then lifted to his her holy eyes,
Wet with the tears of sacrifice.

"Nay, nay," he answered, "there is no need
That the hearts of babes should ache and bleed;
Run away to your bed, and to-morrow play,
You and your pet, through the live-long day."
He laid his hand on her shining hair,
And smiled as he blessed her standing there,
With 'kerchief folded across her breast,
And her small, brown hands together pressed,
A quaint little maiden, shy and sweet,
With her lambkin crouched at her dainty feet.
Away to its place the lamb she led,
Then climbed the stairs to her own white bed,
While the moon rose up and the stars looked down
On the silent streets of Windham town.

But when the heralds of morning came,
Flushing the East with rosy flame,
With low of cattle and scurry of feet,
Driving his herd down the village street,
Young Manning heard from a low stone wall
A child's voice clearly yet softly call,
And saw in the gray dust standing there,
A little maiden with shining hair,
While crowding close to her tender side
Was a snow white lamb to her apron tied.

"Oh, wait!" she cried, "for my lamb must go
To the children crying in want and woe.
It's all I have." And her tears fell fast,
As she gave it one eager kiss—the last.
"The road will be long to its feet, I pray
Let your arms be its bed a part of the way,
And give it cool water and tender grass
Whenever a wayside brook you pass."
Then away she flew like a startled deer,
Nor waited for the bleat of her lamb to hear.
Young Manning lifted his steel-blue eyes
One moment up to the morning skies.

Then raising the lamb to his breast he strode
Sturdily down the lengthening road.
"Now God be my helper," he cried, "and lead
Me safe with my charge to the souls in need.
Through fire and flood, through dearth and dole;
Though foes assail me and war clouds roll,
To the city in want and woe that lies,
I will bear this lamb as a sacrifice."

Bela Elderkin, eldest son of Vine and Lydia Elderkin, was born in Windham, Ct., Feb. 3d, 1770. Susan Bates was born in Nunda, Livingston county, N. Y., March 19th, 1782.

They were married in 1796. They had ten children, six boys and four girls.

Susan Elderkin died at Newtown Flats, on Tionesta Creek, Venango County, Penn'a, Feb. 12, 1826, six days after the birth of her youngest child.

Bela died at Siverlyville, Venango Co., Penn'a, Aug. 3, 1853, aged 83 years.

Bela, when a boy, attended common schools, and spent two terms at the Windham Academy, and then learned the trade of house joiner. He left Windham Aug. 22, 1793, for the far West, which at that time was any place west of the Hudson River. He carried with him the following introduction and recommendation addressed by Hon. Jabez Clark, a prominent lawyer of Windham, to his brothers, Dr. Deodotus Clark and Grastus Clark, attorneys, at Clinton, N. Y.: "Dear Brothers—The bearer of this is Mr. Bela Elderkin, a son of Capt. Vine Elderkin. He is a young man who desires to push his fortune in a new world. By trade a house joiner. I can recommend him freely as promising fair to be a useful man and valuable inhabitant of your country, and desire your friendship and influence in his favour, should he settle in your neighborhood. Any kindness shown to him will be considered as done to your friend and brother."

"JABEZ CLARK."

He continued his course Westward till he reached the Gennesse River, where the town of Nunda was afterward built. Here he married his wife.

His business life was attended with three severe reverses of fortune, which kept him most of the time in limited circumstances. When he had eight children, in April, 1819, he moved into the pine forest of Venango County, Penn'a, where he followed lumbering fifteen years; then moved to Harmony, Chautauqua County, N. Y., where he lived on his own farm till near the time of his death. He spent his last days with his youngest daughter, Mary Siverly, at Siverlyville.

He was honest, truthful, and sedate; a Presbyterian by profession, he was a firm adherent to all the moral teachings of the scriptures and conscience. He was highly esteemed wherever known for his temperance, integrity, veracity, benevolence and virtue.

Susan Bates was the daughter of Phineas Bates and Mary Laraby, who were married in 1781.

THEIR CHILDREN—SEVENTH GENERATION.

NAMES.	BORN.	MARRIED TO.	DATE OF MAR.	DIED.
1 Vine.	Jan. 5, 1797.	Nancy Norton.	Mar. 30, 1826.	Sept. 24, 1864.
2 Lydia.	Nov. 1, 1801.			Dec. 2, 1813.
3 Julia S.	June 17, 1805.	Hiram Kellogg.	1825.	April 10, 1881.
4 Zuba.	Oct. 10, 1807.	John Fleming, Esq.	1823	1866.
5 Clarissa M.	Feb. 5, 1810.	Philip H. Siverly.	May 5, 1831.	Dec. 28, 1894.
6 Phineas B.	Feb. 22, 1812.	Mariah Noble.	July, 1835.	
7 John Bela.	Oct. 13, 1814.	Mary Wallaston.	Feb. 25, 1836.	Nov. 18, 1887.
8 Dyer White.	April 9, 1817.	Cornelia Walker.	July 27, 1842.	
	July 17, 1823.	Cornelia Walker.		June 27, 1854.
	Aug. 31, 1830.	2d Louis King	Aug. 22, 1854.	
9 Ira.	Mar 22, 1822.	Phebe A. Rockwell.	June 15, 1843.	April 21, 1873.
10 Steven W.	Feb. 6, 1826.			

See Chapter VIII. for continued description of this family.

CHAPTER VII.

Mary Anne Elderkin, 2d daughter of Vine and Lydia Elderkin, was born Dec. 18th, 1771. She first married Henry Clark in 1795, by whom she had six children. He died in 1810. The same year she married Dr. James Jackson, and had three children. Dr. James Jackson was born 1778, died 1829. She died July 18th, 1858, at the advanced age of 86 years, 6 months, 22 days.

She was a remarkable woman in many substantial good qualities. Her keen perception and general observation familiarized her with the world, its people, and their virtues and vices. She was active in business, generous and humane to the erring, true to the teachings of Christianity and untiring in her labors for the aged and infirm. Her virtues were inculcated into the minds of her descendants till all seem to know her as a model of greatness and goodness among our ancestors. She was the medium of information among her kindred. Traveling from Connecticut to Illinois, she spread the genial influences and intelligence of her noble mind wherever the ties of consanguinity called her. Her remains rest by the side of her brother, Stephen White Elderkin, at Rose Hill Cemetery, near Chicago.

SEVENTH GENERATION – CHILDREN OF HENRY CLARK AND MARY ANNE (ELDERKIN) CLARK

NAMES.	BORN.	MARRIED TO.	DATE OF MAR.	DIED.
1 Augustus.	Nov. 7, 1795.	Unmarried.		N.Orl'ns 1821
2 Hannah.	July 28, 1797.	Giles Jackson.	Jan. 17, 1818.	Mar., 1867.
		Giles Jackson.		Feb. 14, 1820.
	Nov. 29, 1801.	2. David L. Roberts.	June 2, 1830.	Dec. 30, 1864.
3 Harriet C.	July 31, 1799.	Elias Brewster.	Aug. 8, 1824.	Mar. 16, 18[illegible]4.
	Dec. 30, 1782.	Elias Brewster.		Feb. 19, 1858.
4 Henry.	1803.	Olive Hawks.		
5 Mary Anne.	July 6, 1804.	David L. Roberts.	April, 1828.	Nov. 19, 1829.
		David L. Roberts.		Dec 30, 1864.
6 Louisa E.	1808.	Ephram C. Reed.	Nov. 14, 1825.	May 20, 1837.
		Ephram C. Reed.		Jan. 22, 1859.

SEVENTH GENERATION—CHILDREN OF DR. JAMES JACKSON AND MARY ANN ELDERKIN.

NAMES.	BORN.	MARRIED TO.	DATE OF MAR.	DIED.
1 James C.	March 28, 1811.	Lucretia Brewster.	Sept., 1830.	
	Feb. 25, 1810.	Lucretia Brewster.		
2 Giles W.	May 23, 1814.	Hannah Jennings.		Jan. 31, 1878.
	April 4, 1815.	Hannah Jennings.		April 20, 1883.
3 Jane E.	Aug., 1817.	Elish Leffingwell.	Nov. 26, 1836.	
	Aug., 1850.	Elish Leffingwell.		Feb., 1871.

See Chapter IX for further records of these families.

SIXTH GENERATION.—Stephen White Elderkin, second son of Capt. Vine and Lydia Elderkin, was born Sept. 12th, 1773. He was six feet in hight, and was an extraordinary good man ; but not very energetic. He married widow Mary Powell, and died without children in Jefferson, Ill. Was buried in Rose Hill Cemetery, near Chicago, in 1856, aged 73.

SIXTH GENERATION.—Julianna Elderkin, daughter of Capt. Vine and Lydia Elderkin, was born June 20th, 1776. Married Timothy Staniford, of Windham, Conn. She died Oct. 27th, 1844, leaving one son, James, who married and had one child in 1834.

SIXTH GENERATION.—Lucy Elderkin, daughter of Capt Vine and Lydia Elderkin, born Nov. 27th, 1778. She married Major Joseph Strong. She died in 1819, near Sandusky, Ohio, leaving one daughter, Anna, who married Mr. Neims.

SIXTH GENERATION.—Charlotte Elderkin, daughter of Capt. Vine and Lydia Elderkin, born March 23d, 1781. Married Charles Moseley. In the early part of his life he was a merchant. He died at Ann Arbor, Mich., Dec. 1851. She died in 1866 ; 85 years of age. They left one son, Dunham Moseley, who married and had two children. P. O. address, Anita, Cass County, Iowa.

CHAPTER VIII.

In this chapter the children of Bela and Susan Elderkin, with their families and descendants, will be presented in order down to the present time.

SEVENTH GENERATION.—Dr. Vine Elderkin, born Jan. 5th, 1797.

Nancy Norton, born Sept. 17th, 1793. Married March 30th, 1826.

Vine Elderkin, M. D., died at Ashville, Chautauqua County, N. Y., Sept. 24th, 1864.

Nancy Elderkin died at Ashville, N. Y., Jan. 2d, 1880, 86 years old.

The Doctor was born in Geneseo, N. Y., and graduated in the medical department of Yale College in 1821, a physician and surgeon, and commenced practice in Manlius, N. Y., whence he moved, in 1822, to a place in Chautauqua County, afterward named by his suggestion, Ashville. He was a clear-minded, keen-sighted man; a good judge of character; a thorough and successful practitioner; a law-abiding citizen and an honest man. He and his wife were members of the Congregational Church. Nancy was the daughter of Samuel Norton, of Berlin, Conn., and Phebe Edwards, of Meriden, Conn. She was a very kind, industrious, economical woman, and brought to her husband $12,000 from her father's estate.

THEIR CHILDREN—EIGHTH GENERATION.

NAMES.	BORN.	MARRIED TO.	DATE OF MAR.	DIED
1 Harriet N.	June 24, 1827.			
2 Hiram.	Feb. 8, 1829.			Sept. 17, 1830
3 Mary E.	Mar. 4, 1831.			
4 Jane H.	July 27, 1833.	Wickham Hetfield.	Oct. 25, 1863.	
5 Maria M.	Sept. 24, 1835.			Sept. 15, 1855.
6 Henry.	Oct. 16, 1837.	Loretta Shamp	Jan. 30, 1870.	

(Address, Harmony, Chautauqua County, N. Y.)

The three living daughters of Dr. Vine and Nancy Elderkin reside at the present time, in the old brick mansion of their parents at Ashville. They are educated and noted for their financial ability.

Jane Heart Elderkin married Wickham Hetfield, Oct. 25th, 1863. They are members of the M. E. Church. They own and run two boats on Lake Chautauqua. (Address, Harmony, Chautauqua County, N. Y.

THEIR CHILDREN—NINTH GENERATION.

1. Alton Norton Hetfield, born August 4th, 1864.
2. Elbert Vine Hetfield, born April 26th, 1869.

Henry Elderkin married Loretta Shamp, Jan. 30th, 1870. She is a very mild, amiable, affectionate wife and mother. (Address, Watt's Flats, Chautauqua County, N. Y.)

THEIR CHILDREN—NINTH GENERATION.

1. Vernon H., born June 8th, 1878.
2. Earl L., born June 15th, 1882

SEVENTH GENERATION.—Julia Staniford Elderkin, born June 17th, 1805.

Dr. Hiram Kellogg, born Sept. 20th, 1802.

They were married 1825.

He died Dec 27th, 1878.

She died April 10th, 1881.

Dr. Kellogg settled in Ashville, Chautauqua County, N. Y., where he engaged in mercantile business, which proved unprofitable in so newly settled section of country. He bought a farm, but not being accustomed to labor, he studied medicine and practiced two years in the State of Louisiana. Returning home he depended mostly upon his farm for a living. He was a man of good principles, and belonged to the M. E. Church.

Mrs. Kellogg was a good, noble-minded woman. Her condition in life was not equal to her talent and genuine excellence She bore the principal burden of rearing a large family. Was peaceable, industrious, liberal; firmly attached to family and friends, and highly respected as a Christian woman.

THEIR CHILDREN—EIGHTH GENERATION.

NAMES.	BORN.	MARRIED TO.	DATE OF MAR	DIED.
1 Marcia C.	Feb. 2, 1826.			Nov. 26, 1841.
2 Ulisses H.	May 20, 1828.	Lizzie Wilson.		
3 Albert.	June 7, 1830.	1st, Phebe Shaver.	May 30, 1850.	
	May 26, 1830.	Phebe Shaver.		
	July 12, 1847.	2d, Anna Lin.	Sept. 22, 1870.	
4 Julia Ann.	July 11, 1832.	Edward Morey.	Mar. 4, 1849.	July 27, 1877
	Mar. 11, 1832.	Edward Morey.		
5 Hiram C.	May 21, 1834.			
6 John T.	Aug. 12, 1836.	Lucy L. North.		
		2, Jane M. Lackerby	Oct. 1, 1878.	
7 Susan E.	July 24, 1838.	Richard Comestock.		Dec, 24, 1863.
	July 5, 1832.	Richard Comestock.		Sept. 11, 1864.
8 William E.	May 5, 1841.	Died in U. S. A. Ar'y.		Oct. 27, 1861.
9 Daniel Dy'r.	July 9, 1843.	Died in U. S. A. Ar'y.		May 31, 1863.
10 Lorinda F.	Mar. 18, 1846.	Eugene Post.		Dec. 21, 1867

Ulisses Henry Kellogg, M. D., was a man of great eccentricities of mind and habits, possessing a large share of talent badly directed. It is supposed he died in one of our Western Territories in 1878, where he was acting as secretary and sketcher for a corps of U. S. surveyors. He left a wife and one daughter, Jennie. (Address, Jamestown, New York.)

NINTH GENERATION.

Jennie Kellogg, born March —— 1863.

Rev. Albert Kellogg is a local Methodist minister, now residing in Mishawaka, Ind , where he conducts a furniture store He has been twice married—first to Phebe Shaver, who had five children, second to Anna Lin, who had four children.

NINTH GENERATION—THEIR CHILDREN.

NAMES.	BORN.	MARRIED TO.	DATE OF MAR.	DIED.
1 Alexander.	Oct. 27, 1851.			
2 Anna.	Mar. 1, 1853.			Dec. 24, 1853.
3 Mary.	May 9, 1857.			June 12, 1863.
4 Frank	June 24, 1860.			
5 Freddie.	June 4, 1864.			Sept. 29, 1864.
6 Lily Mary.	Aug. 2, 1873.			Sept. 28, 1874.
7 Ray.	June 13, 1878.			Aug. 28, 1879.
8 Clyde.	June 10, 1880.			July 13, 1880.
9 Emma Grace	Nov. 9, 1881.			

The death rate in this family is remarkable It probably arose from an excessive solicitude of the parents for their children, inducing them to call in their family physician on all occasions of slight attacks of disease.

Julia Ann Kellogg was a large, fine looking woman with light complexion, blue eyes, a clear mind, and kind disposition. Edward M. Morey is a stone mason. (Address Watts Flats, Chautauqua County, N. Y.)

THEIR CHILDREN--NINTH GENERATION.

NAMES.	BORN.	MARRIED TO.	DATE OF MAR.	DIED.
1 Ann Vernetta	Oct. 11, 1850.			Oct. 15, 1855.
2 Alice L.	May 15, 1853	H. H. Slayton.		
3 Olive Lovina	July 17, 1863.	Geo. Chapman.		

Alice L Morey was born May 15th, 1853.

Herman H. Slayton, born Jan. 6th, 1858.

Married, Oct. 29th, 1879.

(Address, Watts Flats, Chautauqua County, N. Y.)

THEIR CHILDREN TENTH GENERATION.

NAMES.	BORN.	MARRIED TO.	DATE OF MAR.	DIED.
1 Sarah L.	Oct. 5, 1880.			
2 Minnie F.	May 27, 1882.			
3 Edward A.	Dec. 1, 1883.			

Olive Lovina Morey married George Chapman, Dec. 10th, 1882. Olive L., born July 17th, 1863. George F. Chapman, born Dec. 20th, 1856. They have one child, Albert Eugene, born Feb. 10th, 1885.

Hiram Clinton Kellogg, born May 21st, 1834. He is a carpenter and joiner, and resides at Forest, Hardin County, Ohio. He married a widow, who has a son and daughter by her first husband.

John T. Kellogg, of Toledo, Ohio, born Aug. 12th, 1836, in the town of Harmony, Chautauqua County, N. Y. He went to Toledo in 1855, where he married Lucy L. North, with whom he lived till 1875. They had one child. In 1861 he enlisted in the Sixth Michigan Infantry, where he held the rank of Orderly Sergeant of Engineers ; pay $34 per month, with clothing and rations. Served 14 months, when he was honorably discharged. Enlisted again in 1864, served five months as First Lieutenant in Co. H, 138th Indiana Volunteers ; and was honorably discharged. October 1st, 1878, he married Jane M. Lackerby, a widowed lady, born and educated at Alston, England. She came to Toledo to visit her brother, George Milburn, then President of the Milburn Wagon Company. Mr. Kellogg spent many years as foreman or contractor of some manufacturing company. He is now in business of his own, keeping an extensive

Livery, Boarding and Sale Stable in Toledo, Ohio. He has a fine residence, a large, four-gabled brick barn, and a brick mercantile block, and is in prosperous circumstances.

HIS SON—NINTH GENERATION.

Wm. A. Kellogg.

Susan E. Kellogg, born July 24th, 1838.

Richard Comestock, born July 5th, 1832.

They were married, 1852.

Susan, died Dec. 24th, 1863.

Richard, died Sept. 11th, 1864.

THEIR CHILDREN—NINTH GENERATION.

NAMES.	BORN.	MARRIED TO.	DATE OF MAR.	DIED.
1 Emmet L.	Oct. 2, 1854.	Emma B. Hadley.	Sept. 1, 1874.	
2 Merit A.	Feb. 19, 1858.	Mary E. Jenner.	July 4, 1880.	
3 Albert W.	May 6th, 1861.			

Susan E. Comestock was an amiable woman, whose virtues and good qualities were many. She was dearly beloved by relatives and acquaintances. Mr. Comestock was a farmer, and an industrious, honest man.

Emmet L. Comestock, born Oct. 2d, 1854.

Emma B. Hadley, born June 23d, 1859.

Married, Sept. 1st, 1874.

(Address, Protection, Erie County, N. Y.)

THEIR CHILD—TENTH GENERATION.

Emerson B., born Nov. 8th, 1875.

Merit A. Comestock, born Feb. 19th, 1858.

Mary Eliza Jenner, born Feb. 15th, 1860.

Married, July 4th, 1880.

THEIR CHILDREN—TENTH GENERATION.

1. Albert Wilber, born July 2d, 1881.
2. Charley David, born April 10th, 1883.
3. Florence Inis, born May 19th, 1885.

Merit A. Comestock is a man of good habits, and has a pleasant lady for his wife. He is a manufacturer of cabinet furniture at Watts Flats, Chautauqua County, N. Y.

SEVENTH GENERATION.—Zuba Elderkin, daughter of Bela and Susan Elderkin, was born in Nunda, Livingston County, N. Y., Oct. 10th, 1807.

John Fleming, Esq., born 1804.

They were married, 1822. Afterwards she had three other husbands.

THEIR CHILDREN—EIGHTH GENERATION.

NAMES.	BORN.	MARRIED TO.	DATE OF MAR.	DIED
1 H.J. Fleming	1823.	Nancy Hoag.		
2 B. Fleming.	1825.	Rachel Walleston.		
3 N H. Fleming	May 7. 1830.	John J. Main.		
4 C. Harrington	1833.			
5 Ira Campbell	1842.			
6 Jos. Campbell	1844.			
7 Flora Allen.	1854.	John Roberts.		

After parting with her first husband, she kept house for her father a number of years. She was industrious, and had some talent, but was a poor judge of the qualities of men. Her first husband was the best of the four. She died in Warren County, Pa., in 1867.

Hiram J. Fleming, born 1823.

Nancy Hoag, born 1835.

Were married, 1854.

THEIR CHILDREN—NINTH GENERATION.

NAMES.	BORN.	MARRIED TO.	DATE OF MAR.	DIED.
1 Millard F.	1851.	Ella Pyles.	May, 1881.	
2 Wallace.	1854.			
3 Thomas.	1856.	Aggie Broadwick.	1881.	
4 Walker.	1862.			
5 Ralph.	June, 1867.			

Of this family, Millard has no children; Wallace has three. He married a lady in Illinois eighteen years old. Thomas has two children. His wife was twenty-seven years old when married. Hiram J. Fleming is a farmer and doctor, height, five feet, ten inches; weight, 170 pounds. His family were raised in Warren County, Pa., whence they removed in 1880 to Kansas, where they now reside. The children are quite intellectual and energetic.

Buel Fleming, born in Forest County, Pa., 1825.

Mrs Rachel (Tuttle) Walleston, born May 7th, 1830.

Married, 1854.

THEIR CHILDREN—NINTH GENERATION.

1. Lafayette, born 1855.
2. George, born 1860.
3. Eleanor I., born 1862.

They lost two or three children, whose names are not known. Mrs. Rachel Fleming, while living with her first husband, had one son, Ebenezer Walleston, who is married and now lives in Bradford, McKean County, Pa. Buel Fleming and his wife Rachel, being incompatible in their organization, parted in 1869, she leaving him in Illinois, returned to Warren County, Pa., bringing her youngest child, Eleanor Irene, with her. After obtaining a bill of divorce, Mr. Fleming married a second wife, and has one son, born 1877. Mr. Fleming is a tall, fine looking man.

Eleanor Irene Fleming, born 1862.

John Hunter, born 1859.

Married, 1880.

(Address, Fagundus, Warren County, Pa.)

THEIR CHILDREN—TENTH GENERATION.

1. Edith Gertrude, born 1881.
2. Carl, born March, 1883.
3. George, born 1884.

Mr. John Hunter is a fine looking man, works at lumbering, is of a kind disposition, and highly respected as a citizen.

Eleanor is tall, slim and full of mental activity and mirth.

Nancy H. Fleming, born in Forest County, Pa., May 7th, 1830.

John J. Main, born in Cattaraugus County, N. Y., June 20th, 1820.

Married, Oct. 1853.

(Address, Grand Valley, Eldred Township, Warren County, Pa.)

Mr. Main died, Nov. 19th, 1878.

THEIR CHILDREN—NINTH GENERATION.

NAMES.	BORN.	MARRIED TO.	DATE OF MAR.	DIED.
1 Lewillin B.	Dec., 1855.			1856.
2 Florence L.	July 3, 1858.			1858.
3 Flora Belle.	March 3, 1860.	1 Geo. T. Flood. 2 James F. Brush.	May 2, 1877. Jan. 2, 1884.	
4 Lafayette M.	May 29, 1867.			

John J. Main was a farmer and a life-long Democrat. During the wild oil land speculation he contracted his farm for $18,000, but before payment the war closed, a terrible flood came, bridges and telegraph wires were swept away, and the mania of the wildest *furore* in a game of chance that the world ever knew came to an end in a day ; so he lost the golden prize.

Nancy is a remarkable woman in many good works. Her disposition is mild, her industry untiring, her work never ending and her patience equal to any emergency. She was unequally yoked, and carried an unequal share of the cares and burdens of life.

Flora B. Main, born in the year 1860, in Eldred Township, Warren County, Pa., was married May 2d, 1877, to

George T. Flood. She had one child by this marriage, Pearl Victoria, born Oct. 22d, 1878. She was married again Jan. 2d, 1884, to James F. Brush, at Grand Valley, Pa., by Rev. W. H. Childs, according to the rules of the U. B. Church. James F. Brush was born in the year 1854. He is six feet tall, and weighs from 171 to 191 pounds. He is good looking and well educated, is a bricklayer, kalsominer and paper-hanger by trade. His people are uncommonly good looking and high-tempered. James and Flora had one child, a little daughter, born April 9th, 1885, Dollie Lin Brush, by name. Both of Flora's children are stout built, with light complexion, light hair, blue eyes and rosy cheeks. They are bright, handsome children.

Charles Harrington, Jr., born, 1833.

He served his country in the War of the Rebellion. He bought and cleared up a farm in Warren County, Pa., removed to Michigan where he purchased a farm and remained two or three years, when he sold out and started for Texas. When crossing the State of Arkansas he was robbed and murdered. He was a bachelor.

Ira Campbell, of Butler County, Pa , is one of two sons of David Campbell by his wife Zuba. At last accounts he owned a coal-mine in Butler county. He is a nice looking man, was married and had one son.

Ira's brother died in the United States army in the War of the Rebellion.

Flora Allen, born about 1852.

John Roberts, born about 1840.

They were married, and live near Chautauqua Lake, State of New York.

Clarissa Mary Elderkin, daughter of Bela and Susan Elderkin, was born in Nunda, Livingston County, N. Y., February 5th, 1810.

Philip H. Siverly, Esq., born September 3d, 1803.

They were married May 5th, 1831.

She died December 28th, 1884.

(Address, Olney P. O., Philadelphia, Pa.)

THEIR CHILDREN—EIGHTH GENERATION.

NAMES.	BORN.	MARRIED TO.	DATE OF MAR.	DIED.
1 Walter.	Jan. 29, 1832.	Lucy L. Dimond.	Dec. 8, 1870.	
2 Emily.	Aug. 29, 1834.			
3 Albert.	June 25, 1836.			May 8, 1837.
4 Caroline.	May 19, 1838.	J. W. McIntire.	Jan. 5, 1860.	
5 Sarah.	Dec. 29, 1841.	J. W. Gardner.	Dec. 24, 1863.	
6 Hamilton.	Mar. 12, 1845.			May 30, 1853.

P. H. Siverly's father was of German descent. He was well educated, and possessed more than ordinary talent. He was one of the pioneer settlers of the Allegheny river, and located at the place now called Siverlyville, where he performed the several duties of farmer, teacher, and Justice of the Peace. He raised eight children, four sons and as many daughters. They were an intellectual family. All the members of this family, parents, children and grandchildren moved to Iowa about 1838, except P. H. Siverly, who located on the old homestead near Oil City. Here he officiated as Justice of the Peace and Recruiting Officer during the War of the Rebellion. He was extensively known as a politician. His friendship, affability, and generosity were appreciated by a large circle of acquaintances. At the time of the great oil land excitement, he sold a portion of his farm for $100,000, and moved to Philadelphia where he now lives at the advanced age of 83 years, retaining his physical and mental powers in a remarkable degree.

Clarissa Mary, his wife, was noted for her industry, family government, unwavering adherence to religion, and moral rectitude; and all the attributes of womanly graces that adorn, embellish and dignify a wife, and qualify a mother to instill into the minds of her children the elements of true greatness and goodness. The result of her maternal discipline and moral example is fully exemplified in the character and rank of her family.

Walter Siverly, born January 29th, 1832.

Lucy L. Dimond, born November 18th, 1841.

Married December 8th, 1870.

(Address, Archie P. O., Venango County, Pa.)

They have no children. Walter Siverly is one of the noted mathematicians of America. He has solved and demonstrated 35 problems hitherto unknown to the world. He has figured largely in petroleum oil and is now a member of the Oil Exchange at Oil City. His industry, integrity and gentlemanly bearings command the respect of all who know him. Mrs. Siverly is worthy of just such a husband.

Emily Siverly is a worthy maiden lady residing with her sister at Siverlyville. She is alike ornamental and useful in every department of life.

(Address, Archie P. O., Venango County, Pa.)

Caroline Siverly, born May 19th, 1838.

J. Watson McIntire, born September 8th, 1838.

Married January 5th, 1860.

THEIR CHILDREN--NINTH GENERATION.

NAMES.	BORN.	MARRIED TO.	DATE OF MAR.	DIED.
1 Blanche.	Mar. 3, 1861.	D. R. Harper, Jr.	Oct. 30, 1883.	
2 Ida May.	Nov. 12, 1862.			

John Watson McIntire died February 12th, 1863. He was a very energetic merchant during his short business life. Mrs. McIntire is a lady of education, refinement and manners.

(Address, Olney P. O., Philadelphia, Pa.)

Blanche McIntire, born March 3d, 1861.

D. R. Harper, Jr., born January 28th, 1856

The Harper family is too well known to require any description in this work. As publishers they have a world-wide fame. Mrs. Harper is well educated and moves in the fashionable circles of Philadelphia.

Business address, 610 Chestnut Street, Philadelphia. Residence at Ridley Park.

Miss Ida May McIntire, born November 12th, 1862.

She is her uncle's idea of a model woman, in height, size, form, and mental endowments. Always active, healthy and helpful toward advancing any good purpose; she is destined to smooth up the rough and broken spots in her path of life, and cast a glow of sunshine upon the dark shadows of the world.

(Address, Olney P. O., Philadelphia, Pa.)

Sarah Siverly, born December 29th, 1841.

J. Wesley Gardner, born March 14th, 1842.

Married, December 24th, 1863.

(Address, Archie P. O., Venango County, Pa.)

THEIR CHILDREN—NINTH GENERATION.

NAMES.	BORN.	MARRIED TO.	DATE OF MAR.	DIED.
1 Harry H.	Sept. 11, 1864.			
2 Maud.	Aug. 2, 1868.			
3 Grace.	Feb. 13, 1873.			
4 Florence I..	July 19, 1883.			

John Wesley Gardner is an active business man, having operated largely in the production of petroleum, as well as in the coal and lumber trade. He is now engaged in the mercantile business at Oil City, Pa., where he is a partner in an extensive lumber yard. He is, in the strictest sense, a gentleman at home and abroad. Mrs. Gardner has a large share of all the good qualities of both her father and mother.

Phineas B. Elderkin, son of Bela and Susan Elderkin, born February 22, 1812.

Mariah Noble, born December 20, 1820.

Married, July, 1835.

Mariah died July 19, 1868.

THEIR CHILDREN—EIGHTH GENERATION.

NAMES.	BORN.	MARRIED TO.	REMARKS.
1 Susan.	Oct. 2, 1839.		Died in infancy.
2 Lorena.	June 28, 1842.	John Brown.	Had 5 children.
3 Andrew.	Sept. 16, 1844.	Flora A. Scott.	Wounded in army.
4 Edward.	July 1, 1847.		Died in U. S. Army.
5 Maritta.	Apr. 20, 1849.	John Vansise.	Had 7 children.
6 Mariah.	June 25, 1851.	George Swift.	Had 3 children.
7 Viletta.	Nov. 17, 1853.	Ephraim S. Rockwell	Lives at Cambridge, Pa.
8 Hiram.	Oct. 25, 1858	Unmarried	Lives in Minnesota.

Phineas Bates Elderkin and his family are farmers. All but one reside in Crawford County, Pa.

John B. Elderkin, son of Bela and Susan Elderkin, born October 13, 1814.

Mary Wallaston, born August 3, 1811.

Married February 25, 1836

Mary Elderkin died November 12, 1868.

John B. Elderkin married Orilla King, April 20, 1871.

(Address, Grand Valley, Warren County, Pa.)

CHILDREN BY FIRST WIFE—EIGHTH GENERATION.

NAMES.	BORN.	MARRIED TO.	DATE OF MAR.	DIED.
1 James W.	Dec. 23, 1836.	Josina Stanton.	July 3, 1865.	
2 Samuel C.	Aug. 23, 1838.	H. Houghtaling.	Apr. 24, 1864.	
3 Jane H.	Apr. 26, 1840.	John Franklin.	Jan. 2, 1853.	
4 Oliver C.	Apr. 11, 1842.	Emma Johnson.		
5 Phebe S.	Aug. 24, 1844.	Thomas Smith.		
6 John B., Jr.	Aug. 18, 1846.	In the	Union Army	Aug. 2, 1864.
7 George B.	Aug, 18, 1846.			Aug. 15, 1847
8 Mary E.	Mar. 19, 1849.	Geo. Peas.	Jan. 27, 1865.	
9 Garrett D.	Apr. 28, 1851.	Martha Buchanan.	Dec. 1879.	
10 Susan A.	June 16. 1854.	J. Vosburg.		

John Bela Elderkin is a farmer. About the beginning of the War of the Rebellion he built a lumber mill, and ran it during the great oil excitement at Titusville, and till the death of his wife in 1868. His children are all farmers.

James W. Elderkin, born December 23, 1836.

Josina Stanton, born May 12, 1844.

Married July 3, 1865.

(Address, Ackley Station, Warren County, Pa.)

THEIR CHILDREN—NINTH GENERATION.

NAMES.	BORN.	MARRIED TO.	DATE OF MAR.	DIED.
1 Elbert L.	March 11, 1866.			
2 G'enni C.	March 17, 1877.			

James W. Elderkin is an industrious, thrifty farmer. He is very pleasant and agreeable in his manners.

Samuel C. Elderkin, born August 23, 1838.

Harriet Houghtaling, born March 10, 1846.

Married April 24, 1864.

(Address, Grand Valley, Warren County, Pa.)

THEIR CHILDREN—NINTH GENERATION.

NAMES.	BORN.	MARRIED TO.	DATE OF MAR.	DIED.
1 Lilian D.	Sept. 5, 1865.			
2 Minnie A.	June 17, 1868.			
3 John A.	July 24, 1870.			
4 Emma G.	July 30, 1878.			
5 Clinton.	Feb 5, 1884.			

Samuel has a family of bright children : his own health has been poor most of his life. Disposition kind and generous.

Jane H. Elderkin married John Franklin. They had two children, Walter and Flora.

Oliver C. Elderkin, born April 11, 1842.

Emma Johnson, born —— ——

Married —— ——

(Address, Bonair, Howard County, Iowa.)

They have one beautiful little daughter. Oliver is a great worker, and has earned money enough in the oil district of Pennsylvania to make him rich, but he lacks the faculty or desire to keep it. His motto is "but one life to live ; live it as you go."

Phebe S. Elderkin, born August 24, 1844.

Thomas Smith, born February 29, 1848.

Married September 8, 1877.

(Address, Grgnd Valley, Warren County, Pa.)

THEIR CHILDREN—NINTH GENERATION.

NAMES.	BORN.	MARRIED TO.	DATE OF MAR.	DIED.
1 Albert Ward.	Sept. 20, 1878.			
2 Evie.	Dec. 31, 1880.			
3 Bina Mae.	May 8, 1883.			

These children are bright, intellectual, well developed and handsome.

Garret Demill Elderkin, born April 28, 1851. An orderly, energetic, thrifty farmer.

Martha Buchanan, born 1861.

Married December, 1879.

(Address, Bonair, Howard County, Iowa.)

Mary Elizabeth Elderkin, born March 19, 1849.

George Peas, born —— ——.

Married January 27, 1865.

(Address, Fredericks, Chickasaw County, Iowa.)

THEIR CHILDREN—NINTH GENERATION.

1. Cora. 2d. John. 3. Edward.

Susan Alzina Elderkin, born June 16, 1854.

Jerry Vosburg, born —— ——.

Married —— ——.

Mr. Vosburg died in 1878.

They had no children. Mrs. Vosburg is a very amiable lady. In 1886 she married Albert McKee, and lives now at Friendship, N. Y. They have one son.

Dyer White Elderkin, son of Bela and Susan Elderkin, born April 9, 1817.

Cornelia Walker, born July 17, 1823.

Lois King, born August 31, 1830.

Cornelia W. Elderkin, died June 27, 1854.

Married to Cornelia Walker, July 27, 1842.

Married to Lois King, August 22, 1854.

(Address, Spartansburg, Crawford County, Pa.)

THEIR CHILDREN—EIGHTH GENERATION.

NAMES.	BORN.	MARRIED TO.	DATE OF MAR.	DIED.
1 Mary Jane.	April 27, 1843.	Francis Doud.	Jan. 23, 1860.	Oct. 28, 1867.
2 Sarah F.	Nov. 23, 1845.	Rollin C. Clark.	May 3, 1866.	
3 Emily C.	June 21, 1847.	L. L. Deming	July 1, 1872.	
4 Ellen A.	April 23, 1849.	C. L. Deming.	May 12, 1874.	
5 Walker W.	July 31, 1851.	Mary J. Stanton.	Oct. 16, 1877.	
6 Ward King.	July 27, 1855.	Mary E. Shute.	July 6, 1876.	
7 Ida Lois.	Aug. 18, 1857.	Murray H. Warren.	Aug. 11, 1877.	
8 Rhoda C.	Feb. 6, 1859.	Z. T. Whitehill.	Feb. 14, 1878	
9 Flora B.	Oct. 5, 1860.			
10 Minnie B.	Dec. 19, 1862.	Milton D. Stone.	Sept. 8, 1886.	
1 Dyer W.	Sept. 12, 1864.			

Dyer W. Elderkin is the eighth child of Bela and Susan Elderkin. He was born in Nunda, Livingston County, N. Y., April 9, 1817. When he was two years old his parents moved to Tionesta, Venango County, Pa., where the lumbering business was the principal employment of the family for fifteen years. When he was but nine years old, his mother died, leaving six children at home, of whom Mary was the eldest, and Stephen W., an infant seven days old. That noble-hearted sister cared for the family seven years, when she married P. H. Siverly and took her young brother with her to her own home.

Dyer W., when a boy, was prompt, fearless, truthful and observing. He was called by the neighbors both "Deacon" and "Colonel."

After contesting the title to a tract of land three years, Bela Elderkin was beaten and lost his home, with a heavy bill of costs, at Tionesta. In 1834 the remnant of the family moved to a farm near Ashville, Chautauqua County, N. Y., which had been purchased while in the lumber woods. Dyer W. soon became noted for his rapid acquisition of scientific knowledge. While taking his academical course at Jamestown, N. Y., on the stage and in the lyceum, he was both envied and admired. On the 18th day of August, 1840, he was appointed Captain in the 162d Regiment of Infantry, of the State of New York, under Wm. H. Seward. He found his company on the extreme right of the Regiment; but after two years' drill was promoted to No. 2 in the Regiment. He was well adapted to command; height, five feet, ten inches, with a clear, strong voice and patriotic spirit, inherited from the fathers of the Revolution; a strong, electric brain battery, coupled with a tendency to speech-making, gave to him an unlimited control over his company. In September, 1840, he commenced the study of law in the office of Judge Marvin. During the last four months in school he had studied fifteen hours a day, which impaired his health and led to a consumptive condition. He left the office and took lodging with his eldest brother, Dr. Vine Elderkin, who, with counsel, treated him, and finally decided the case hopeless. He went home to his father's expecting to die soon. A very trifling observation suggested to his mind a method of treatment which rapidly restored health again; and introduced a train of thought which, in riper years, resulted in the development of his new theory of consumption, "Its Origin, Progress and Cure." His natural diathesis, being opposed to a sedentary life, led him into the more active pursuits of the people of that period, when our country was mostly a forest, and its industry principally clearing land. He bought and partly cleared four different farms: then engaged in mercantile business four years; then manufactured scythe snaths three years; then planned and carried through a land lottery scheme. He taught school in the States of New York, Pennsylvania and Kentucky. While teaching a class in Astronomy in the South, he discovered the origin, uses and ends of Comets and Planets, and the eternal perpetuity of the stars which are all suns. In 1854, while residing at Columbus, Warren County, Pa., he was elected Justice of the Peace and commissioned by

Wm. Bigler, Governor. He resumed the study of law at the same time. He officiated as Justice of the Peace four years, when he bought a farm joining the borough of Spartansburg, where he has resided to the present time, farming and practicing law alternately, as business presented itself. Born a Whig, and being a great lover of human rights, he assisted in organizing the Republican party and was very active in sustaining the Government during the Rebellion. Science has always predominated over finances in his organization, creating a desire for original research. He read Dwight's Theology and studied the scriptures carefully. He read medicine incidentally all along the early part of his life, and at the age of fifty-three, procured a small medical library, which he read at intervals for ten years, for the purpose of knowing how much that valuable profession knows, and how much remains unknown. He has often been heard to express surprise that with all the ignorance and disadvantages of our ancestors—with their continued habit of being repeaters, they ever brought so much light out of total darkness as they did. Second. With all the advantages of the glowing light of science shining upon the pathway of our contemporaries, the development of truth is so slow. Philosophy, Astronomy and Nature, in their causes and effects, have furnished themes of pleasing research for his hours of leisure. A few of his original theories on different subjects are submitted to the readers in the last part of this book.

He was first married at the age of twenty-five years to Cornelia Walker, with whom he lived twelve years, and they had five children. Second marriage to Lois King, who has six children. The first wife was five feet, one inch in height, and weighed one hundred and ten pounds. She was educated and possessed an amiable disposition, a keen, penetrating mind, extraordinary memory, and a remarkable parental government. She never spoke an angry word during her married life. She was too frail and too good to remain long in this world. She left four little daughters and one son to be cared for by the unknown " Ma." that might take her place.

The second wife is five feet, seven inches in height, and at the time of marriage weighed 180 pounds. Has been strong, healthy and energetic in labor and business. She is highly esteemed by all her acquaintances; and has demonstrated the great problem: " Can a step-mother be as kind to step-children as to her own?" How gratifying the memory of those years of kindness must be to her, when those happy children return on a visit to the old home, always bringing to " Ma." rich presents as tokens of love and respect. Her own children are not behind in their manifestations of love and esteem.

Mary Jane Elderkin, born April 27, 1843.

Francis Doud, born April 5, 1839.

Married January 23, 1860.

Mary J. Doud died October 28, 1867.

Francis Doud died October 18, 1877.

THEIR CHILDREN—NINTH GENERATION.

1. James Freemont, born September 10. 1861. Died November 4, 1875.

2. Velma Grace, born November 21, 1864.

Mary J. Doud, in her mental qualities and characteristics, as well as in size and height, resembled her mother very closely.

Francis Doud was a man of more than ordinary business talent He married a second wife by whom he had three children.

Miss Velma Grace Doud resides with her great uncle, Wm. Walker, who raised and educated her. Her opportunities have been excellent, and she has improved them to her advantage. She is a successful teacher at the present time.

(Address, Bear Lake, Warren County, Pa.)

Sarah Francis Elderkin, born November 24. 1845.

Rollin C. Clark, born October 15, 1837.

Married May 3, 1866.

Rollin C. Clark died January 30, 1884.

(Her present address is Mrs. Fannie S. Clark, No. 108 Columbia Street, West New Brighton, Staten Island, N. Y.)

THEIR CHILD—NINTH GENERATION.

Rollie Marie, Born August 12, 1875.

Rollin C. Clark was raised in the vicinity of Titusville, Pa. When oil was first discovered he engaged in speculations in that product, and soon accumulated $10,000, which he invested in a drug store at Titusville. He compounded and manufactured the medicine known as "Clark's Anti-Bilious Compound," in company with his brother, C. S. Clark. He was well known in the business circles of Cleveland, O. He engaged, in company with Murray H. Warren, in oil-producing and refining in the Bradford oil field, where, by his business reputation and the energy of his partner, they were financially successful.

At the time of Mr. Clark's death the company owned one of the finest oil refining works in the United States, located at Corry, Erie County, Pa., with a branch at Baltimore.

Sarah Frances, *alias* Fannie S. Clark, was born at Bear Lake, Warren County, Pa., immediately after the return of her parents from Kentucky. She was a brilliant young lady, with high aspirations, and a restless, roving disposition. Mr. Clark's means were ample and she was gratified with every desire for accomplishments and traveling. She spent one year in the Elocution School of Boston, where she became an excellent sensational speaker. She practiced upon the stage in the city of New York one year, and took lessons in music in Cleveland several years. She visited all the places of notoriety in the United States. Finally her nervous system yielded to her overwrought efforts, and she sought retirement at her home on Staten Island. Her daughter Rollie is with her; a nice little girl.

Emily Caroline Elderkin, born June 21, 1847.

Loton L. Deming, born April 17, 1825.

Married July 1, 1872.

(Address, Charleston, Franklin County, Arkansas.)

THEIR CHILD—NINTH GENERATION.

Maud Uphema, born July 28, 1873.

Loton L. Deming has a son by a former wife, Charles L. Deming. At one time he owned a large ranche in California. Afterward lumbered, and manufactured doors, blinds, etc., in Pennsylvania. He lost most of his property in the hard times which followed the war. His occupation is now farming and stock-breeding.

Emily C. Deming used to teach school. In music, she is an extra vocalist. She is a fine artiste. Maud is a bright little girl.

Ellen Amelia Elderkin, born April 23, 1849.

Charles L. Deming, born December 24, 1850.

Married May 12, 1874.

(Address, Rocklio, Placer County, Cal.)

THEIR CHILDREN—NINTH GENERATION.

1. Claire Winfield, born June 16, 1876.

2. Lenox Edwin, born July 18, 1879.

3. Lillian Amelia, born July 19, 1881. Died April 15, 1885.

Charles L. Deming is a kind and patient husband and father. He graduated at the Commercial College at Erie, Pa. He is a natural mechanic, an engineer, and can run and repair any kind of machinery.

Ellen A. Deming is smart and quick, a good conversationalist, attends church regularly, and always teaches a class in Sunday School. She is neat, tidy, and an excellent housekeeper.

Walker White Elderkin, born July 31, 1851.

Mary Jane Stanton, born July 7, 1861.

Married, October 16, 1877.

(Address, Nos. 271 and 273 Frankstown Avenue, East End, Pittsburgh, Pa.

THEIR CHILDREN—NINTH GENERATION.

1. Goldie Florence, born March 7, 1879.

2. Mable Cornelia, born June 8, 1882.

3 Mary Jane, born September 5, 1884.

W. W. Elderkin was born in Columbus, Warren County, Pa., while his father was engaged in mercantile business. At the age of six years he displayed the tendencies of his mind by trafficking with his schoolmates. At fourteen he took a span of fine horses from Oil City to Philadelphia, a distance of four hundred miles. When seventeen, during the great oil excitement in Western Pennsylvania, he butchered and sold meat, poultry, butter, etc., in Titusville, clearing $1,000. At twenty he opened a hardware store in Spartansburg, where he did a successful business for three years. Thinking the place too small for his aspirations, he sold out and went West—as far as Dakota. Here he remained one year. Finding the population too sparse, it seemed like keeping hotel in the woods, so he bought a farm, for luck, and returned to the oil region, where he engaged in the grocery business at Edenburg. He remained at this town three years, till the floating population drifted to Bradford, when he sought a more stable class of customers at his present location in Pittsburgh. He is a success, socially and financially. His integrity, honesty and energy are the cornerstone of his prosperity. His attachment to home, family and friends is very strong.

Mary, his wife, is an excellent woman, a descendant of one of our noted families.

Ward King Elderkin, M. D., born July 27, 1855.

Mary Elizabeth Shute, born ———

Married July 6, 1876.

(Address, Chautauqua, Chautauqua County, N. Y.)

THEIR CHILD—NINTH GENERATION.

Dimonda Susabelle, born May 5, 1880.

Dr. Ward K. Elderkin, in his early boyhood, indicated the tendency of his mind by making bread pills and preparing vials of berry juice, with which he acted the part of doctor at the children's play-houses. He graduated at the Eclectic Medical Institute of Cincinnati in 1881, with the honors of Physician and Surgeon. He immediately entered his field of practice at Riceville, where he had a liberal share of the town and country patronage. His superior success in the healing art demonstrates the importance of adapting organization to business. He is a deep thinker and a close reasoner; discards all ostentatious display, and seeks success only through genuine merit.

Mary E. Elderkin is an English lady of active mind and remarkable memory, whose parents reside in Cleveland, Ohio.

Ida Lois Elderkin, born August 18, 1857.

Murray H. Warren, born September 27. 1854.

Married August 11, 1877.

(Address, Corry, Erie County, Pa.)

THEIR CHILDREN—NINTH GENERATION.

1. Laura Blanche, born July 3, 1881.

2. Murray Heller, born January 25, 1883.

Murray H. Warren is a descendant of a well known family, who are prominent in the military, political and medical history of the United States. Partaking of the spirit of his ancestors, he is fearless and daring amidst dangers, prolific in resources in great emergencies, far-seeing in the possible events of the future, and commanding in his deportment. A first-class financier, his generosity extends almost to profusion.

A gentleman in business and demeanor, he can conduct a difficult or dangerous enterprise with more skill and certainty than most operators. He is now President of the Pennsylvania Oil Company, Limited, of New York City and Chicago, which company was organized as a medium of distribution for Clark & Warren's oils. Mr. Warren oversees the entire business, and has immediate charge of the refining works located at Corry and Baltimore.

Mrs. Warren is a woman of firm characteristics; height, five feet, five inches; weight, 156 pounds, with fine form and face, well adapted to her sphere in life.

Rhoda Cornelia Elderkin, born February 6, 1859.

Z. T. Whitehill, born July 18, 1851.

Married, February 14, 1878.

(Address, Knox P. O., Clarion County, Pa.)

THEIR CHILDREN—NINTH GENERATION.

1. Minno Pearl, born June 29, 1879.

2. Charles Freemont, born January 16, 1881.

Zachera T. Whitehill was born and reared at Edenburgh, Clarion County, Pa. He is six feet, two inches in height, fine looking, and of a commanding appearance. Has been engaged in oil producing since arriving at his majority. He has shared the vicissitudes of fortune common to oil producers. When fortune smiles he cannot retire; when misfortune casts its dark shadow around, he sees no route to eminence so short as a gushing well. So he continues in the same business.

Mrs. Rhoda C. Whitehill combines all the qualities and virtues that constitute a genuine lady. Height, five feet, three inches; weight, 136 pounds; features regular, plump and fine looking; disposition, kind.

Miss Flora Belinda Elderkin, born October 5, 1860.

(Address, Spartansburg, Crawford County, Pa.)

Her fashionable taste, style and order excel in everything she does. Height, five feet, three inches; weight, 126 pounds; fair looking; light complexion and brown hair.

Minnie Belle Elderkin, born December 19, 1862.

Milton D. Stone, born —— ——.

Married September 8, 1886.

(Address, Jamestown, Chautauqua County, N. Y.)

Mrs. Minnie B. Stone is five feet, five inches in height, and weighs 150 pounds. Is strong, energetic and self relying. She expresses her opinions frankly. She can be relied on in all the vicissitudes of fortune.

Milton D. Stone is one of Corry's noblest young men; well educated and well bred, he is intellectual moral, energetic, honest and methodical. His perceptive powers readily scan surroundings, conditions and results so that he is always found on the right side of financial questions. He is in the employ of the Chautauqua County National Bank, at Jamestown, N. Y., and owns an interest in a large tract of timbered land.

(Address, Spartansburg, Crawford County, Pa.)

Dyer Webster Elderkin, born September 12, 1864.

Height, five feet, ten inches; weight, 170 pounds. He is strong, healthy, energetic and honest; is an unceasing worker, conducting the affairs of a large farm at the present time. Besides the branches of a common school education, he has studied Algebra, Natural Philosophy, Astronomy and Physiology. He is pleasant and affable in his manners, and would make a reliable clerk or partner in a heavy mercantile business.

Ira Elderkin, son of Bela and Susan Elderkin, born March 22, 1822.

Phebe Ann Rockwell, born June 26, 1826.

Married, June 15, 1843.

Ira Elderkin died April 21, 1873.

THEIR CHILDREN—EIGHTH GENERATION.

NAMES.	BORN.	MARRIED TO.	DATE OF MAR.	DIED
1 Alfred W.	Aug. 9, 1844.	Killed in the army.		Sept. 20, '63.
2 Elizabeth J	June 24, 1846.			April 29, '49.
3 Angeline J.	May 3, 1847.	Lost 3 husbands Lives in Texas.		
4 Mary Ann.	Nov. 19, 1851.			May 15, '54.
5 Harriet E.	Feb. 12, 1854.	1. Eugene Phelps. 2. Ewd. Baungrass.		
E. Phelps	was killed by a	car in 1882.		
6 Sarah Jane.	July 19th, 1856.	1 Frank Service. 2 Fred Ecker.		
7 Vina C.	Aug. 12, 1862.	James B. Terry.		
8 Adda Dell.	Sept. 7, 1864.	Budd White in Texas		
9 Jas. Russel.	Dec. 1868.	Address, Watts Flats Chautauqua Co., N. Y.		
10 George Ira.				June 20, '64.

Ira Elderkin was a farmer. He was noted for his physical strength, agility and musical talent. He was a good husband, kind father and faithful friend. His jolly organization was the centre of merriment in all the social circles of his acquaintance.

Phebe Ann Elderkin was a true helpmate, always at her post, during her husband's lifetime. She, by her untiring energy, raised and educated their minor children after his death

(Address, Watts Flats, Chautauqua County, N. Y.

The children of Ira Elderkin are brilliant and mirthful. They seek change of place and employment. Angeline conducted successfully a laundry in Denver, Col. Has now a ranch in Texas, at Gainsville, Cook County. Harriet is at the same place; also Adda. Their husbands are, engaged in raising and feeding stock. Vina C. Terry is the wife of a railroad contractor, at Meadville, Crawford County, Pa. Jennie Ecker lives at West Flats, Chautauqua County, N. Y. James R. Elderkin is a wild boy with an active mind and strong will power, which, if properly directed, will make a mark in the world. His eye is on railroading.

Stephen W. Elderkin, born February 6th, 1826.

Address, Olney P. O. Philadelphia, Pa.

He had a slender constitution and poor health during the early part of his life. He has remained single, and has always lived with his brother-in-law, P. H. Siverly.

CHAPTER IX.

Hannah Clark, daughter of Henry and Mary Ann Clark, born July 28, 1797.

Married January 17, 1818.

Giles Jackson died February 14, 1820.

THEIR CHILD—EIGHTH GENERATION.

Sarah Atwood Jackson, born 1820.

Died August 23, 1832.

David L. Roberts, born November 20, 1801.

Married Hannah, widow of Giles Jackson, June 2, 1830.

David L. Roberts died December 30, 1864.

Hannah Roberts died March, 1867.

THEIR CHILDREN—EIGHTH GENERATION.

NAMES.	BORN.	MARRIED TO.	DATE OF MAR.	DIED.
1. Mary Anne.	June 7, 1831.			
2. Jane.	Feb. 28, 1833.			March, 1834.
3. Ellen O.	May 6, 1835.			Dec. 8, 1873.
4. Roderick.	June 6, 1837.			June 21, 1840.
5. Glendower.	Oct. 23, 1841.			Oct. 2, 1842.

The history of this family is unknown to the writer, but one fact, which should not be overlooked, appears that their generosity knew no bounds.

Mary Anne Roberts, the only surviving member of the family, appears to be a woman of culture and refinement, with a mind capable of original investigation and decision. Many thanks to her for the information furnished for this work.

(Address, 690 W. Monroe street, Chicago, Ill.)

Mary Anne Clark, daughter of Henry and Mary Ann Clark, born July 6, 1804.

David L. Roberts, born November 20, 1801.

Married April, 1828.

She died November 19, 1829.

He died December 30, 1864.

THEIR CHILD—EIGHTH GENERATION.

Clark Roberts, born November 12th, 1829.

Lizzie Linscott, born ——.

Married, ——.

THEIR CHILDREN—NINTH GENERATION.

1. Charles N.
2. Lewis C.
3. Willis H.
4. Ella.
5. Linscott.
6. Mary Otteline.

Hon. Elias Brewster, born December 30, 1782.

1. Lucretia Edgerton.

2. Harriet Clark, born July 31, 1799.

Lucretia Edgerton married May 8, 1807. Had four children.

Harriet Clark married August 8, 1826. Had seven children.

Hon. E. Brewster died February 19, 1858.

Lucretia Brewster died ——.

Harriet Brewster died March 16, 1874.

THEIR CHILDREN—EIGHTH GENERATION.

NAMES.	BORN.	MARRIED TO.	DATE OF MAR.	DIED.
1. Lucretia E.	Feb. 25, 1810.	James C. Jackson.	Sept., 1830.	
2. Silas W.	Jan. 4, 1813.	Mary A. Walden.	April 27, 1837.	
3. Sarah E.	Feb. 1, 1815.			July 24, 1837.
4. Samuel W.	June 23, 1821.			June 20, 1830
5. Henry A.	June 8, 1827.	Arminda Baily.	June 9, 1862.	
6. Elias Pinco	Apr. 24, 1829.	Chas. A. Dittrick.	Mar. 21, 1856.	Jan. 4, 1865.
7. Harriet H.	May 14, 1831.	Marshall C. Fuller.	May 30, 1857.	
8. Sardius C.	Oct. 23, 1833.	Sarah A. Gaylord.	July 17, 1862.	
9. Elliott P.	Dec. 27, 1836.			April 15, 1838.
10. Mary Jane.	Jan. 3, 1840.			
11. Roderick P.	Dec. 3, 1842.	Sarah F. Thomas.	Dec. 10, 1865.	

" Hon. Elias Brewster was born in Columbia, Windham county, Conn., was a lineal descendant of Elder Wm. Brewster, 'Chief of the Pilgrims,' and a very reputable offspring from that worthy ancestry. He lived in his native town until manhood, after which he spent several seasons teaching on Long Island. He then located at Mexico, Oswego county, N.Y., in 1809, where he lived until his death—a period of nearly half a century. During most of that time he held some public office, as Town Clerk, Justice of the Peace, Supervisor for many years, County Treasurer, County Judge, and Member of Assembly. All these offices he filled with *ability, honesty* and *integrity.* He was an easy and gifted public speaker, and could present his thoughts with so much clearness, logic and pathos as to carry an audience to the same concluding point where he arrived. He was a kind father, an affectionate husband and benevolent neighbor. His business faculty enabled him to rear and educate a very large family of children. But the crowning excellence of Judge Brewster was his Christian character. He united with the First Presbyterian Church of Mexico in the spring of 1832, and was soon after chosen a ruling Elder, which office he held until death, performing its duties in a faithful and satisfactory manner. He loved the Church of Christ, the Bible, the Christian Sabbath, the house and worship of God, and the Prayer meeting. He evinced a clear understanding of the fundamental principles of Christianity, and the doctrine of the Cross, and in his life exemplified their practical tendency. He adhered to them, and when there was need 'contended earnestly for the faith once delivered to the saints.' He was a judicious, exemplary, useful Christian man. The writer visited him the last afternoon of his life. With great difficulty of utterance he expressed his strong confidence in Christ as the rock on which he planted his feet and cast the anchor of his soul. Thus he lived, and thus he died in the faith and hope of the Gospel; and, as we doubt not, is now enjoying the 'rest that remaineth to the people of God.'"

OBITUARY.

"In Irving, Nebraska, March 16, 1884, Mrs. Harriet C. Brewster died, aged 75 years.

"Harriet Clark Brewster was born in Manlius, N. Y., July 31, 1799. She was married August 8, 1826, to Elias Brewster, and removed to Mexico, Oswego county, where she lived until 1858, when, her husband having died, she came with her children to Florence, Neb., and the next year to Irving, in the same State. Here she lived till she passed to the home above. Converted in her childhood, hers was one of those quiet, earnest, faithful Christian lives, which always exercise an abiding influence on those who come in close contact with them. Her sphere was her home. It was here her patient, self-denying love was manifest. The mother of seven children, she gave much of her life in loving service for them, and was rewarded by seeing them all come in youth into the fold of Christ. Nor was her interest confined to her own. All who came to her home shared her kindness and sympathy. Her life was a continued outgoing of love and good deeds—of doing for others. Her religious experience was deep and strong, and full of faith and fervency. During the last years of her life, when the writer knew her, it was a special privilege to converse with her on religious topics. Her mind found its chief delight in the things of the Bible, which to her was the book of books.

"Her death was caused by cancer, and she was a great sufferer, especially during the last few months. She often expressed the desire that she might be kept from all murmuring; and her patient, uncomplaining deportment was a marvel to all. In no place, perhaps, does it require more grace to live for God than in intense physical pain, when it would be far easier to die than to live; and they who go triumphantly through this to the glory of the life beyond, leave behind them the strongest possible witness to the sustaining grace of their Savior. Such witness has she left to us,—to the many who mourn her loss. A faithful, devoted wife and mother and friend, beloved by all who knew her, Grandma Brewster (as she was familiarly called in the neighborhood), will long be remembered, and many will be better for having known her. She rests from her labors and her works do follow her." T. W. DeLong.

Note.—For the general genealogy of the Brewster family see page —, chapter X.

Henry Clark, born ——, 1803.

Olive Hawks, born ——, ——.

Married, —— ——.

THEIR CHILDREN—EIGHTH GENERATION.

NAMES.	BORN.	MARRIED TO.	DATE OF MAR.	DIED.
1 Charlotte M.	May 24, 1825.	Salem Town.	May 19, 1845.	
2 Augustus	1827.	Maria J. Cross.		
3 Mary Anne				7 years old.
4 Maria H.	March 19, 1835.	Geo. F. Carlisle.	March 19, 1857.	
5 Henry, Jr.				In childhood.

Charlotte Maria Clark, born May 24, 1825.

Salem Town, born ——.

Married, May 19, 1845.

THEIR CHILDREN—NINTH GENERATION.

NAMES.	BORN.	MARRIED TO.	DATE OF MAR.	DIED.
1.				In infancy.
2.				In infancy.
3. Otteline.		Wm. Davis.		

They reside in California.

Augustus Clark, born 1827.

Maria Josephine Cross, born ——.

Married, ——.

Maria Josephine died, leaving one daughter.

Maria Hawks Clark, born March 19, 1835.

George F. Carlisle, born October 19, 1830.

Married March 19, 1857.

G. F. Carlisle died 1865.

THEIR CHILDREN—NINTH GENERATION.

1. George.
2. Ada.
3. Edward.

Louisa E. Clark, daughter of Henry and Mary Ann Clark, born 1808; died May 20, 1837.

Ephriam Carpenter Reed, born —— ; died Jan. 22, 1859.

Married Nov. 14, 1825

THEIR CHILDREN—EIGHTH GENERATION.

1. Helen Amelia, died in infancy.

2 Louisa Mary, died in infancy.

3 Mary Louisa, born Nov. 20, 1833; married Wm. E. Clark, M. D., Dec. 26, 1865.

Dr. Wm. E. Clark, born Feb. 22, 1819.

Mary Louisa Reed, born Nov. 20, 1833.

(Address, 690 West Monroe street, Chicago, Ill.)

THEIR CHILDREN—NINTH GENERATION.

1. William E., Jr., born May 7, 1867.

2. Grace, born February 28, 1869.

William E. Clark, M. D., is a graduate from the School of Regular Physicians, a descendant from the family of Windham, Conn., Clarks. Jabez Clark was a prominent lawyer of Windham, Conn. He married Amie Elderkin, seventh child of Col. Jedediah Elderkin. Jabez Clark had two brothers located at Clinton, N. Y., in 1793—Dr. Deodotus Clark and Grastus Clark, attorney-at-law. Dr. William E. Clark is now one of 918 practicing physicians in the great city of Chicago.

Dr. James Jackson, born 1778. Died, 1829.

Mary Ann Elderkin, born December 18, 1771. Died July 18, 1858.

They were married in 1810.

THEIR CHILDREN—SEVENTH GENERATION.

NAMES.	BORN.	MARRIED TO.	DATE OF MAR.	DIED.
1. James C.	March 28, 1811.	Lucretia E. Brewster	Sept. 1830.	
2. Giles W.	May 23, 1813.	Hannah Jennings.		Jan. 31, 1878.
3. Jane E.	August 23, 1817.	E. Leffingwell, M.D.		

James C. Jackson, M. D., born March 28, 1811.

Lucretia Edgerton Brewster, born February 25, 1810.

They were married September, 1830.

(Address, Dansville, Livingston county, N. Y.)

THEIR CHILDREN—EIGHTH GENERATION.

NAMES.	BORN.	MARRIED TO.	DATE OF MAR.	DIED
1. Mary.				In infancy.
2. George.				Early manh'd
3. James H.	June 11, 1841.	Kate Johnson.	Sept. 13, 1864.	

Extract from a lecture delivered by James C. Jackson, in Liberty Hall, March 28, 1881, the day he was seventy years old:

"I was born of goodly stock. My paternal grandfather was Col. Giles Jackson, of Tyringham, Berkshire county, Mass., who was at the battle of Saratoga, and had the honor of engrossing the articles of capitulation of General Burgoyne. Col. Jackson was the father of twenty-one children, of whom my father was the fifteenth Longevity and large size were characteristics of the family; but from ante and post-natal causes my father was, when born, feeble, and grew sickly, and was, when grown up, sick and small in size, never weighing more than one hundred and twenty-four pounds. My father's brothers were all large men, weighing from one hundred and seventy-five pounds to two hundred and twenty, and ranging from five feet eight inches to six feet two inches in height; three or four of the sisters were five feet ten to eleven, and one, six feet, so I have been told, and all were finely proportioned.

"My mother was a magnificent person. The humor in her large and rich, and the woman in her paid it reverent obeisance. No one who knew her thought of her first because of her sex. She was so large in her intellectual endowments and had such great spiritual conferments, that she always, on all general occasions, kept the merely feminine qualities in her out of sight. These were reserved, as I think, rightly, for her husband and children and special domestic relationships. Her grandfather was Colonel Jedediah Elderkin, a great revolutionary patriot, known in Connecticut's historical collections as of 'bull-frog memory.' She, too, came of longevious ancestry, and of large, robust stock. I have never known a hardier, handsomer, and naturally a more capacious woman than she was; and this view of her was taken by all her contemporaries."

James C. Jackson is so extensively known that anything the writer of this work could say would add nothing to his popularity. He began his career of medical life under the auspices of the old allopathic school, where every symptom of disease was met by a counteracting force, which had a direct tendency to destroy the vital forces of the patient, and rendered his recovery more hazardous than no treatment at all. Depletion was the first great object sought. This was accomplished by vivesection, cathartics, emetics, universal solvents and opiates. The wholesale slaughter of human life produced by that theory and practice of medicine, then, as it is even unto this day, was too shocking to his organization to be followed for the mere purpose of a livelihood. From the Puritan fathers he had inherited the noble qualities, honesty, justice, humanity, love, sympathy and generosity; also a deep, clear, penetrating mind, which gave to him the power to be an original thinker and actor. From his standpoint he surveyed the medical world in all its acts and effects; and groaned, grieved, wept and prayed for a brighter light and a safer road to the realm of earthly health and life. With one firm determination of mind, he dashed from his pinnacle into the abyss below the whole drug theory. He then inquired of nature: What is health? What is disease? How is health perpetuated? How is disease induced? These questions furnished food for long, deep, original thought and investigation. He began his hygienic practice about 1844. In 1856 he established a home cure or sanitorium on the hillside at Dansville, N. Y., where he has received and treated over 20,000 patients. His theory was a puzzle to the medical world, but his success in healing the sick has been astounding. He cures by bringing invalids into a direct line of nature's laws. He is the author of several pathological and hygienic works, and has published a "Health Journal" about thirty years. The Sanitorium has grown to be a magnificent establishment, capable of providing for 500 patients at the same time. He is now retired with a liberal competency. The present proprietors are James H. Jackson, M. D., Albert Leffingwell, M. D., E. D. Leffingwell, M. D., and Wm. E. Leffingwell, Sec. and Treas.

James H. Jackson, born June 11, 1841.

Kate Johnson, born April 7, 1841.

They were married Sept. 13, 1864.

(Address, Dansville, Livingston county, N. Y.)

THEIR CHILD—NINTH GENERATION.

Arthur, born May 4, 1868.

James H. Jackson may well be a splendid man, circulating, as he does, in his veins, the blood of such an ancestry as Rev. Stephen White, Col. Jedediah Elderkin, Col. Giles Jackson and Judge Elias Brewster. With such antecedents we may look for a consequential man, like Dr. James H. Jackson, full of energy in business, a profound thinker and ready writer, with a desire for the welfare of mankind as broad as the world. He was born in Petersburg, Madison county, N. Y. His wife, in Sturbridge, Mass.

(Address, Dansville, Livingston county, N. Y.)

Arthur Jackson is a young man with promising ability, attending school at this time.

Giles W. Jackson, son of Dr. James and Mary Ann Jackson, born May 23, 1813. Died January 31, 1878.

Hannah Jennings, born April 4, 1815. Died April 20, 1883.

Married. ——.

THEIR CHILDREN—EIGHTH GENERATION.

NAMES.	BORN.	MARRIED TO.	DATE OF MAR.	DIED.
1. Henry A.	June 12, 1837.	Caroline Rathbun.	June 23, 1881.	
2. Lizzie.	Nov. 30, 1840.	George B. Morgan.	1866.	
3. James.				In infancy.
4. Harriet.	Sept. 23, 1847.	Chas. M. Catlin.	1871.	

Giles W. Jackson was born May 23, 1813, at Manlius, Onondaga county, N. Y. He died at the age of 64 years, 8 months and 8 days, in Ottawa, La Salle county, Ill. In early manhood he was a clerk in the store of Mr. Fleming, afterward with Mr. Smith, who was a remarkable man for system and order in conducting his business. He had in 1833 an interest in his father's estate of $1,000. With this he intended to engage in the mercantile pursuit. In 1836 he went west, stopping one year at Joliet, Ill. Then he located on a farm three miles north of Marseilles, in the town of Manlius, Ill., which was named at his suggestion after his native place in the State of New York. Here he remained seventeen years, engaged in active industry; when, in 1854, he removed to Ottawa and engaged in the hardware business as the senior member of the firm of Jackson & Lockwood, in which he was eminently successful. He retired in 1873 with a handsome competence. He held many offices of honor and importance, to-wit: Supervisor of the town of Manlius, Supervisor of the County Poor, Member of the Board of Education, and member of the City Council; in all of which he acquitted himself with remarkable acceptance and ability. For nearly twenty years he was superintendent of the county asylum, where his skill and efficiency could not be surpassed. It seldom happens to one to be so universally respected and esteemed as was Giles W. Jackson. His happy family circle attested his domestic virtues. The church cherished his examples and sought his advice. In the different public trusts filled by him, no doubt ever arose in regard to his ability, judgment or unswerving integrity. He embraced the adage, "act well your part; there all honor lies." He embraced the Christian faith when young, and was very zealous in advocating its doctrines. His motto was, "Seek first the Kingdom of Heaven and its righteousness, and all things will be added thereto." All who knew him mourned his loss. At his death the city council, fire company, and other organizations to which he belonged, passed resolutions of condolence. Thus lived and died one of our noblest citizens.

Henry A. Jackson, born June 12, 1837.

Caroline L. Rathbun, born August 17, 1844.

Married June 23, 1881.

(Address, Kirksville, Adair county, Missouri.)

Henry Augustus Jackson was born on a farm near Ottawa, Ill. During his minority he was a dutiful, industrious and kind son to his parents, and an indulgent brother to his two younger sisters. He went to Kansas in 1870, where he engaged in fruit-raising and mercantile business for ten years, successfully. In 1880 he went to Dansville, N. Y., where he was married and remained till June, 1882. In 1883 he purchased his present home, to-wit: the Parcels House, in Kirksville, Mo., a town of about 2,000 inhabitants. His height is five feet seven inches, weight 145 pounds, with light brown hair. He is active, energetic and agreeable; owns the most valuable hotel in the town, and gives his customers the most hospitable reception The characteristics of his father are deeply rooted in his organization

Mrs. Caroline L. Jackson was born at Poplar Ridge, in Cayuga county, N. Y. Height, 5 feet 5 inches; weight, 140 pounds; hair, light brown; complexion, brunette. Her father was a farmer, now living with her, 84 years old. His sister is in the same family, 98 years old, both well and enjoying life.

George B. Morgan, born ——.

Lizzie Jackson, born November 30, 1840.

Married 1866.

(Address, 3899 Washington avenue, St. Louis, Mo.)

THEIR CHILDREN—NINTH GENERATION.

1. Henry, born March 31, 1867.
2. Mabel, born February, 1875.

Mr. G. B. Morgan is a gentleman of a keen, shrewd business tact; the owner of a large amount of real estate in St Louis. He is also extensively engaged in mining in Arizona.

Of Mrs. Lizzie Morgan we can say nothing from lack of acquaintance and information, except from a knowledge of her blood. That tells its story of merit through ten generations. I will risk the assertion that she is endowed with all the amiable qualities of her ancestors.

Charles M. Catlin, born May, 1846.

Harriet Jackson, born September 23, 1847.

Married 1871.

(Address, 688 West Monroe street, Chicago, Ill.)

THEIR CHILDREN—NINTH GENERATION.

1. Carrie, born April 15, 1872.
2. Howard, born November 3, 1876.

I have no clue to Mr. Catlin's business or his wife's qualities. Presume they are all right.

Jane E. Jackson, daughter of Dr. James and Mary Ann Jackson, born August 23, 1817.

Elisha Leffingwell, M. D., born August 28, 1805. Died February 10, 1871.

Married November 26, 1839.

(Mrs. Leffingwell's address is Dansville, Livingston county, N. Y.)

THEIR CHILDREN—EIGHTH GENERATION.

NAMES.	BORN.	MARRIED TO.	DATE OF MAR.	DIED.
1. Albert.	Feb. 13, 1845.	Mary C. Hathaway.	Dec. 23, 1871.	
2. Arthur E.	Sept. 13, 1846.			Sept. 10, 1870.
3. James J.	Sept. 7, 1847.			Sept. 20, 1854.
4. Elisha Dyer.	June 1, 1849.		~~1884~~	
5. William.	July 10, 1855.	Mannie Parke.	Dec. 31, 1878.	

Elisha Leffingwell, M. D., was born at Middleton, Vt. He settled at Aurora, N. Y., where he followed his profession until the time of his death. I have no means of judging of his ability only by his family. He leaves three sons, who from their superior development and capabilities, attest the nobility of their father.

Jane E. Leffingwell was born in Manlius, Onondago county, N. Y., when the country was new and settlement sparse. Schools were few, and educational privileges of a low grade; yet, notwithstanding all the disadvantages of her surroundings, she made rapid progress in procuring a first-class common school education. Her father died when she was twelve years old, leaving her to the guidance of her mother and eldest brother, James C., who was but eighteen. They had a farm, which was sold about four years later, when Jane E. engaged, I think, in teaching, which she followed for a livelihood until her marriage. She was finely developed in form and features, gentle, kind, affectionate and winning in her manners, firm and self-reliant in self-government and the direction of her own pecuniary affairs. She proved to be an amiable wife and a tender, kind mother. She is now sixty-seven years old, enjoying good health and an active mind. She is just fleshy enough to smooth up all the wrinkles and lend a fresh, rosy tint to as beautifully a molded face as our genealogy can boast of. Her home is at the Sanatorium, where her presence reflects the genial influence of her noble heart upon the weak and weary, inspiring hope and confidence in obedience to the laws of life.

Albert Tracy Leffingwell, M. D., born February 13, 1845.
Married Mary C. Hathaway, December 23, 1871.
(Address, care of "Long Island Historical Society," Brooklyn, N. Y.)

Albert Leffingwell, M. D., was born at Aurora, N. Y., and at the age of sixteen left home to support himself. In 1866 he became an instructor at the Polytechnic Institute, Brooklyn, where he taught several years, entering meantime Hamilton College, N. Y., but never graduating. Receiving his medical degree from Long Island College Hospital in 1874, he spent some years in extended travels and studies in Europe and Asia. From 1882 until 1888 he was one of the proprietors of the "Sanatorium," Dansville, N. Y. Dr. Leffingwell has given considerable attention to literature, contributing to the London "Contemporary Review," July, 1880; "The Century," 1880; "Archives of Medicine," 1882; "Lippincott's," 1884; "Popular Science Monthly," 1880; and to other magazines. One work, upon "Vivisection," was published in this country and England in 1889. His wife died September 29, 1886, and he resides at present in London, England. (See also Walworth's "Hyde Genealogy" for ancestry of the Leffingwell family.)

Elisha Dyer Leffingwell, M. D., born June 1, 1849, at Aurora, N. Y. He graduated at Cornell University in 1871, and at Bellevue Hospital Medical College in 1877. The same year he went abroad, where he remained two years. In 1879 he returned and settled at Dansville, N. Y. He is a splendid mathematician, having spent in his early manhood a portion of his time in studying civil engineering. He is a self-made gentleman and scholar, and thoroughly versed in his profession. He is, also, a very fine looking man. He is one of the proprietors of the Sanatorium, at Danville, New York.

William Leffingwell, born July 10th, 1855, at Aurora, N. Y. He is the youngest of five children. He was married to Mannie Parke, December 31st, 1878. He is also a proprietor in the Sanatorium at Danville, N. Y., and is Secretary and Treasurer of that institution. Mrs. Mannie P. Leffingwell was a very sweet and dear little woman. She died after a protracted illness, September 18th, 1883. January 6th, 1885, William Leffingwell married for his second wife, Eliza Nicola, of Cleveland, O. They have one daughter, Mary Anna, born January 16th, 1886.

CHAPTER X.

BREWSTER GENEALOGY.

Elder William Brewster was born in England in 1560. He landed on the Mayflower, with one hundred and ten companions, at Plymouth Rock, December 11th, 1620, at the age of 60 years. His wife's given name was Mary. He knew no fear except the fear to do wrong. His love of right expanded every energy of his soul to such an extent that no barrier could prevent the execution of those duties which he owed to his God and fellowman. He resided at Plymouth and Duxbury from 1620 to 1644. He raised a family of five children, and died April 16th, 1644, at the age of 84 years.

THEIR CHILDREN—SECOND GENERATION.

NAMES.	BORN.	MARRIED TO.	DATE OF MAR.	DIED.
1. Jonathan.	1593.	Lucretia ——		1659.
2. Patience.		Thomas Prince.	1624.	1634.
3. Fear.		Isaac Allerton.	1625.	1633.
4. Love.		Sarah Collier.	1634.	1650.
5. Wrestling.		Unmarried.		Young.

Of these children but little is known. Thomas Prince, the husband of Patience, was at one time Governor of the Colony of Massachusetts. Fear's son, Isaac Allerton, Jr., graduated at Harvard in 1650.

Love Brewster married Sarah Collier in 1634.

THEIR CHILDREN—THIRD GENERATION.

NAMES.	BORN	MARRIED TO.	DATE OF MAR.	DIED.
1. Sarah.		Benjamin Bartlett.	1656.	1691.
2. Nathaniel.				1676.
3. William 2d.	1640.	Lydia Partridge.		Nov. 3, 1723.
4. Wrestling 2d	1642.	Mary Partridge.		Jan. 1, 1697.

Love Brewster inherited his father's homestead at Duxbury, Mass., where he occupied the same house that was occupied by his father.

William Brewster 2d married Lydia Partridge.

THEIR CHILDREN—FOURTH GENERATION.

NAMES.	BORN.	MARRIED TO.	DATE OF MAR.	DIED
1. Sarah.	Apr. 26, 1674.	Caleb Stetson.	1704.	
2. Nathaniel.	Aug. 8, 1676.	Mary Develly.		
3. William 3d.	May 4, 1681.	Hopestill Wadsworth.		Dec. 6, 1768.
4. Lydia.	Feb. 11, 1684.			
5. Mercy.	Dec. 7, 1685.			
6. Benjamin.	July 7, 1688.			
7. Joseph.	Mar. 17, 1693.			
8. Joshua.				

William Brewster 2d resided at Duxbury, Mass.

William Brewster 3d married Hopestill Wadsworth.

THEIR CHILDREN—FIFTH GENERATION.

NAMES.	BORN.	MARRIED TO.	DATE OF MAR.	DIED.
1. Oliver.	July 16, 1708.	Martha Wadsworth.		
2. Ichabod.	Jan. 25, 1710.	Lydia Barstow.		1797.
3. Naomi.	1712.			
4. Elisha.	Oct. 29, 1715.	Lucy Yeomans		1789.
5. Seth.	Dec. 20, 1720.	Jerusha ——		
6. Lot.	Mar. 25, 1723.			
7. Huldah	Feb. 20, 1726.	John Goold.		Apr. 25, 1750.

William Brewster 3d was born and raised at Duxbury, Mass., but finally settled at Lebanon, Ct. His wife belonged to a family noted in the military and financial history of this country.

Oliver Brewster married Martha Wadsworth.

THEIR CHILDREN—SIXTH GENERATION.

NAMES.	BORN.	MARRIED TO.	RESIDENCE.	DIED.
1. Wadsworth.	1737.	Jerusha Newcomb.	Lebanon, Ct.	Mar. 30, 1812.
2. Ruba.		Henry Bliss.	Springfield, Mass.	

Oliver Brewster was born July 16th, 1708. He lived at Lebanon, Ct, and at Barnardstown, Mass. His wife was an authoress. He died at an unknown age. His brother Ichabod lived to the age of 86 years. His father, William 3d, to the age of 87 years; his grandfather, William 2d, to 83 years; his great-grandfather's age unknown; his great-great-grandfather to the age of 84 years. Mrs. Martha Brewster's parents are unknown to the writer.

Wadsworth Brewster married Jerusha Newcomb.

THEIR CHILDREN—SEVENTH GENERATION.

NAMES.	BORN.	MARRIED TO.	DATE OF MAR.	DIED.
1. Oliver 2d.	Apr. 2, 1760.	Jerusha Badger.	1781.	Feb. 15, 1812.
2. Sabra.	Dec. 6, 1761.	Unmarried.		Mar. 20, 1842.
3. Joseph W.	Feb. 23, 1764.	Louisa Badger.	1788.	Sept. 6, 1849.
4. Silas.	" 12, 1767.	Ruby Durkee.		" 30, 1808.
5. Jasper.	June 22, 1769.	Theodosia Lymann.		Dec. 19, 1822.
6. Lydia M.	May 7, 1772.	Daniel Lyman.	1793.	Feb. 29, 1864.
7. Ruby	July 18, 1776.	Jesse Ladd.		July 21, 1824.
8. Jerusha.	Aug. 10, 1779.	Sebra Loomis.	1806.	Apr. 3, 1864.
9. Elias.	Dec. 30, 1782.	1. Lucretia Edgerton	May 8, 1807.	Feb. 19, 1858.
		2. Harriet Clark.	Aug. 8, 1826.	Mar. 10, 1874.
10. Sardius.	Sept. 3, 1785.	1. Harriet Wait.		Apr. 18, 1866.
		2. Julia Clark.		
		3. Eleanor Knox.		

Of this family, Oliver 2d was located at Becket, Mass., was a surgeon in U. S. A. He practiced medicine 33 years, and died at the age of 52.

Sabra died at the age of 80.

Joseph Wadsworth lived in Onondaga, N. Y. Died at the age of 85.

Silas resided at Columbia, Ct. Died at the age of 44.

Jasper located at Madison, O. Died at the age of 53.

Lydia Martha Lyman lived at Manchester, Ct. Died at the advanced age of 91, leaving three daughters and four sons.

Ruby, of Madison, O., died at the age of 48.

Jerusha, of Cazenovia, N. Y., lived to the age of 84. She left three daughters and three sons, one of whom was a missionary.

A description of Judge Elias Brewster will be found on page 76.

Sardius located at Mexico, N. Y. He was a physician and a man of extra ability and moral worth. He died at the age of 80 years. He had two daughters and two sons; one a doctor, the other a lawyer.

Wadsworth Brewster, their father, died at the age of 74.

The family of Hon. Elias Brewster continued:

Lucretia Edgerton (Brewster) Jackson has proved to be a patient, faithful wife and mother. She has walked side by side and hand in hand with her husband in building up his great medical reform and Sanatorium. It has required a vast amount of labor and self-denial; but she still lives to see the grand results of their efforts. See page 81.

Silas Wadsworth Brewster, born January 4, 1813. He was eldest son, by first wife, of Hon. Elias Brewster. Mary A. Walden, born May 10, 1811. He married Mary A. Walden April 27, 1837.

THEIR CHILDREN—NINTH GENERATION.

NAMES.	BORN.	MARRIED TO.	DATE OF MAR.	DIED.
1. Elias W.	Sept. 3, 1838.	Mary W. Barnard.	Mar. 9, 1863.	Sept. 17, 1882.
2. Emeline S.	Oct. 11, 1840.	Unmarried.		June 25, 1844.
3. James B.	Feb. 18, 1844.	"		Feb. 26, 1861.
4. Wadsw'th J.	Feb. 10, 1846.	Anna A. Doud.	Feb. 10, 1867.	
5. Lucretia E.	Nov. 27, 1847.	Unmarried.		

Silas Wadsworth Brewster was born in the town of Mexico, Oswego county, N. Y., in 1813, and was a lineal descendent from Elder William Brewster, who was one of the Mayflower colony that landed at Plymouth in 1620. After graduating at Mexico Academy (at the age of 12 years), he remained some time at home, but in 1833 went to Oswego and clerked for a time in the store of George Deming. In 1835 and 1836 he was connected for one year in the publication of an anti-slavery paper at Utica, known as the "Emancipator of Human Rights." In 1836 he started in the mercantile business in Hannibal, N. Y., with Mr. George Deming as partner. Their place of business was in an old wooden building on the corner of Cayuga street. After five years Deming sold out to H. H. Bronson. Four years later Mr. Bronson withdrew, leaving the business to S. W. Brewster, who, after a few years, erected a three-story brick building in place of the old store. Mr. W. H. Wiggins, who had been a faithful clerk in Mr. Brewster's employ for 18 years, was admitted as partner in 1867. To accommodate their rapidly increasing trade, Mr Brewster purchased a large three-story brick building. The large amount of business wore upon the constitution of Mr. Wiggins so rapidly that he retired in 1870, when Wadsworth J. Brewster was taken as a partner under the firm name of "S. W. Brewster & Son," which continued for about twelve years—to the time of the father's death, which was on the 13th of September, 1882. His life's business was unusually successful and prosperous. He worked with unabated zeal and ambition up to his seventieth year, when his health failed, and he was compelled to leave the responsibility of his immense business in charge of his son, Wadsworth J. Brewster.

He was not a seeker of notoriety by his many acts of charity, but rather in a quiet way assisted in pushing forward many notable reforms. He worked diligently in the anti-slavery reform; was a life member of the American Bible Society, and the temperance society He was for forty years a member of the Presbyterian Church. During his business life there never was a time when the word or name of Silas W. Brewster was not as good as a government note. He was visited a few days before his death by two of his brothers, to wit: Henry A. Brewster, of St. Paul, Minn., and Sardius C., of Omaha, Neb All the business houses in Hannibal were closed during the funeral services in honor of their worthy and much-esteemed citizen.

Hon. Elias Walden Brewster, born September 3d, 1838.

Mary W. Barnard, born April 27th, 1836.

Married March 9th, 1863.

E W. Brewster died September 17th, 1882.

He was born in Hannibal, Oswego county, N. Y., where he spent the early part of his life in school and in assisting his father in his store; but his health failing from asthma, he went to Colorado in 1860, where he cultivated a large garden one year, then returned to his home, where he was married and remained until the spring of 1872. when he moved to Denver, where he remained until his death. He possessed a very fine, well-trained and methodical mind, and was one of the world's most noble and genial men. He first came into prominence in public when the Hon. John L. Rouett was appointed Governor of the territory of Colorado. Then he was made Deputy Secretary of State. When the first State administration was established he was retained in this position by Secretary Wm. H Clark. After the expiration of Mr. Clark's term, he was engaged in the department of Secretary of State to continue the records and compile the State laws. The work of the last Legislature (1881) was prepared for the press by him. When he was taken sick, he was assisting Prof. Shattuck, the Secretary of the State Land Board, in the State Land Office. Mr. Brewster was best known through his kindness and goodness of heart, thoroughly unselfish and generous to a fault. His connection with the State house and public life was marked throughout by deeds of charity to the needy, and sacrifices to his friends that will be long remembered. He had the acquaintance and esteem of the bar of the State, the members of which will deeply regret the loss of so valuable a man. His public work was of a superior character. His Index of the Colorado Code of Laws was pronounced by the best lawyers and judges the best code index ever made in the United States, with the exception of the California code. He died at the age of 44 years and 14 days, in Denver City, of gastric fever, after an illness of seven weeks. His remains were removed and interred in the old cemetery at Hannibal, N. Y. They lost an infant son about 18 years ago, in 1866.

His excellent wife, Mary W. Barnard Brewster, was the daughter of Edward H. and Lydia W. Barnard, of Hudson, N. Y She was born at Germantown, N. Y. Her mental ability, education and refinement place her in the front rank of society. She was married to John Hewlett on the 20th of February, 1885.

(Address, No 64 East 110th Street, New York.)

John Hewlett, born —— ——

Mary A. Barnard Brewster, born April 27th, 1836.

Wadsworth J. Brewster, born February 10th, 1846.

Amy A. Doud, born January 30th, 1844.

Married February 10th, 1867.

(Address, Hannibal, Oswego County, N. Y.)

THEIR CHILDREN—TENTH GENERATION.

1st. Infant son, born July 7th, 1871, died July 9th, 1871.
2d. Birney N., " Sept. 29th, 1873, " March 27th, 1874.
3d. Mabel A., " Oct. 8th, 1877.
4th. Lucretia E., " April 24th, 1882.

Mabel A. has dark hair and eyes like her mother.

Lucretia Edgerton has light hair and eyes like her father.

Both bright, healthy and good looking.

It would require a volume to present a full biographical account of W. J. Brewster and wife and their business transactions. They are both shrewd, energetic persons who find no barriers in business which they cannot surmount, no object to accomplish which they lack influences to push forward to completion They are equal partners in business, and both pull together on the same end of the rope. They are the proprietors of one of the most magnificent mammoth stores, in a country town, in the United States. It was established by S. W. Brewster in 1836. It now resembles a large bee-house with many lodges. One may first enter a first-class grocery, pass on into a room 65 feet deep, crowded with all that pertains to a dry goods store, and with all the customers that can swarm around the counters In one department is an immense display of boots and shoes, sufficient to cover the feet of all the inhabitants of Oswego county. Passing through another door, one almost wonders if all the external sunshine had by magic been directed into this one room. It was flooded with sunbeams and song birds. On looking around for the fairy god-mother, she is seen in a little woman with hair and eyes like night. She is the wife and partner of the male branch of the establishment. On one side is the jeweler's department, where clocks, watches and silverware of all kinds are exhibited, as well as gold chains, bracelets and band. On the other side is the drug store. In the next room may be found a book and stationery stock, covering the entire wants of the trade. The opposite side is filled with queensware, crockery and glass. The glassware is a perfect wonder in color and shape, and the lamps look as though they might shed abroad light enough when well filled, to guide the feet of erring mortals into paths of peace. In the second story of this extended building may be found lace curtains, curtains of damask, with window cornice and poles; also carpets, oil cloths, organs, sewing machines and other articles that nothing short of an invoice could present to the mind of a stranger. The area of floor used in this house is nearly 10,000 square feet. In addition to the immense business referred to, W. J. Brewster & Co. conduct a large banking business. They draw drafts on any business house in the United States, and buy and sell drafts on New York; collect and buy drafts and checks on banks and banking houses in any part of the world.

Mrs. Amy Doud Brewster is the daughter of William H. Doud, who was born, lived and died in Luzerne county, Pa., and his wife, Emily Millie, who was born near Providence, R. I. She was born in Lenoxville, Luzerne county, Pa. Her mother died when she was but seven years old. W. J. and his little Amy D. we will jot down for a representative couple in the Brewster line.

Henry Augustus Brewster, born June 8th, 1827.

Arminda Baily Brewster, born ——

Married June 9th, 1862.

(Address, St. Paul, Minnesota.)

THEIR CHILDREN—NINTH GENERATION.

NAMES.	BORN.	MARRIED TO.	DATE OF MAR.	DIED.
1. Harry B.	Aug. 14, 1864.			Aug. 26, 1865.
2 William.	Feb. 13, 1870.			

Henry A. Brewster was born in Mexico, Oswego county, N. Y. He is the eldest child of Judge Brewster by his second wife, Harriet Clark, she being the connecting link between the White, Elderkin and Brewster families. Her mother, Mary Anne Elderkin, was the daughter of Vine

Elderkin and Lydia White, daughter of Rev. Stephen White, of Windham, Ct. Henry A. had the advantages of a common school education, with a partial course in the Academy of Mexico, and one year in the Grand River Institute of Austinburg, Ohio. He designed, when a young man, to pursue a professional course of life, but not being possessed of a physical constitution adapted to sedentary habits and a close mental application, he turned his attention to hotel keeping, in which business he has been very successful. His height is about 5 feet 8 inches, and weight 145 pounds—a small man with a great heart. Imbued with the noble sentiments of his ancestors, he has proven himself worthy of the high standing he has attained in the first circles of society. He is a member of the Presbyterian church and officiates as an elder. His attachment to family, home, relatives, friends and country are unusually strong and enduring. We cannot better describe this gentleman than to quote the following lines:

"A truthful soul, a loving mind,
Full of affection for mankind,
A helper of the human race,
A soul of beauty and of grace;
A spirit firm, erect and free,
That never basely bends the knee;
That will not bear a feather's weight
Of slavery's chain, for small or great;
That truly speaks from God within,
And never makes a league with sin;
That snaps the fetters despots make,
And loves the truth for its own sake;
That worships God and Him alone,
And bows nowhere but at His throne;
That trembles at no tyrant's nod,—
A soul that fears no one but God,
And thus can smile at curse and ban;—
This is the soul of this kind man."

Mrs. Arminda Baily Brewster is a lady of more than ordinary talent and personal appearance. She is large and commanding in her deportment, being 5 feet 8 inches in height, and weighing 165 pounds. Her ease of address and amiable manners attract the attention of all around her. Her financial ability and ready perception adapt her eminently to the duties of a landlady. In the social and benevolent circles she is a leader and example of generosity and refinement.

> "This world she makes happy, and then beyond this,
> She points to another all sunny with bliss."

Elias Pineo Brewster, born April 24th, 1829.

Charlotte A. Diettritch.

Married March 21st, 1856.

(Her address, Grand Island, Nebraska.)

He died January 4, 1865.

THEIR CHILDREN—NINTH GENERATION.

NAMES.	BORN.	MARRIED TO.	DATE OF MAR.	DIED.
1. Sardius H.	July, 1857.			
2. Bertie P.	Sept., 1863.			

Elias Pineo Brewster, Esq., was an attorney-at-law, who had a bright and hopeful future before him. His circle of friends throughout the State was large. Had his life been spared to his three score and ten years there is no doubt of his having won a national reputation. He died at the age of 35 years, leaving his amiable widow and two young sons to battle with the world without the aid of so able a guardian.

Harriet Hellen Brewster, born May 14th, 1831.

Marshall C. Fuller.

Married May 30th, 1857.

(Address, Irvington, Douglas County, Neb.)

They have no children.

Mrs. Fuller was city missionary for Omaha a number of years, but her health failed so as to compel her to abandon her work. She is at this time (1885) an invalid, residing with her brother, R. P. Brewster. She is resigned to the Master's will even when suffering excruciating pain. Her life is a constant witness for Christ She is a person to whom anyone would look for sympathy in an hour of trial or sorrow. Her faith and patience are a constant example of what the love of Jesus can do for His loved ones. Her height is 5 feet, weight 100 pounds.

Sardius Clark Brewster, born October 23d, 1833.

Sarah A. Gaylord.

Married July 17th, 1862.

(Address, Irvington, Douglas County, Neb.)

THEIR CHILDREN—NINTH GENERATION.

NAMES.	BORN.	MARRIED TO.	DATE OF MAR.	DIED.
1. Hattie L.	Feb. 12, 1864.			
2. Ernest L.	Aug. 12, 1865.			
3. Minnie L.	Aug. 12, 1867.			Dec. 23, 1867.
4. Silas R.	Oct. 4, 1870.			
5. Nellie Hope.	Sept. 20, 1872.			
6. Mary L.	June 2, 1877.			
7. Clarence G.	Sept. 9, 1880.			

Sardius Clark Brewster was born at Hannibal, Oswego County, New York, where he received his education. He went to California when he was twenty years old, where he worked in the mines five years, returning home in 1858, a short time after his father's death. In the fall of the same year he went to Nebraska with his mother, youngest sister and brother. The country was then new, and settlers of various grades of intellectual development and moral influences were pouring in. It was then and there that the influence of the Brewster family was felt in the organization of society. The Puritan sentiment was promulgated by them and other like families, securing the erection of churches and school houses, and the establishing of Sabbath schools.

Mr. Brewster was two years a member of the State Legislature, where his services were highly appreciated. He is one of the men of Nebraska who cannot be bought. He is marked with that peculiar characteristic of his ancestry—honesty.

Farming has been his principal business, in which he has been reasonably successful. Mrs. Brewster is a daughter of Rev. Reuben Gaylord, who was the first Congregational minister in Nebraska, and one of the first in Iowa, and for many years Superintendent of Missions in Nebraska and Western Iowa.

He has accomplished a work that will be of indescribable benefit to that new country. His daughter, Mrs. Brewster, is not unworthy of so noble a parentage She established the first Sabbath school in Omaha It was held in her father's dwelling house, where she was superintendent, chorister and teacher. Omaha has now a population of 60,000, with its scores of steeples piercing the sky, and its many-toned bells ringing out upon the ambient air, "People, come to the house of prayer." Their eldest daughter, Hattie L., is now in the third year of her collegiate course at Oberlin, Ohio, preparatory to her future work as a foreign missionary. She is a talented and noble young lady. Time must develop the future of the younger members of their brilliant family.

Mary Jane Brewster, born January 3, 1840.

(Address, Irvington, Douglas County, Nebraska.)

She is unmarried and lives with her brother, Sardius C. She is five feet in height and weighs 100 pounds. She possesses an estate in her own right of considerable value.

Roderick P. Brewster, born December 6, 1842.

Sarah F. Thomas, born November 7, 1844.

Married December 10, 1865.

(Address, Irvington, Douglas County, Nebraska.)

THEIR CHILDREN—NINTH GENERATION.

NAMES.	BORN.	MARRIED TO.	DATE OF MAR.	DIED.
1. Elliott E.	Dec. 3, 1866.			
2. Roderic E.	Oct. 7, 1868.			
3. Henry C.	June 20, 1870.			
4. Clyde R.	Oct. 26, 1872.			
5. Zerepha F.	May 7, 1875.			
6. Francis E.	Nov. 7, 1876.			April 2, 1879.
7. Paul R.	Dec. 25, 1881.			
8. Edith E.	May 7, 1884.			

Roderick Plymouth Brewster was born at Hannibal, New York His height is five feet eight inches, weight 150 pounds. He is a farmer by occupation, with homestead well improved and pleasant surroundings. His industry and enterprise enable him to provide for and educate his large family of bright, promising children. He is the eleventh child of Hon. Elias Brewster.

His family record closes the entire record of the descendants of Captain Vine and Lydia Elderkin, including all the intermarriages, male and female, with a few exceptions of persons not found.

CHAPTER XI.

This chapter will present the descendants, in one line, so far as they are known, of Bela Elderkin, second son of Col. Jedediah Elderkin.

Bela Elderkin was born December 10, 1751, at Windham, Connecticut. He graduated at Yale College 1767, and was for a time, it is said, engaged in trade in Windham. Previous to this, however, and soon after the breaking out of the Revolutionary war, he was appointed lieutenant of marines on board the ship of war then owned by the State of Connecticut. What service he rendered in this capacity, if any, we are unable to say It was probably soon after his father purchased the mill privilege there that he removed to Willimantic, and lived in a dwelling, now gone, known to the last generation as the "How House," which stood directly across the street from the old grist mill. Here he lived a number of years, and for a time kept a hotel. It is probable, too, that he had charge of his father's business, including the mills in this part of the town. He was living here, it seems, according to his father's will, in 1702. Here, it is probable, most of his children were born. At the time that Wm. L Weaver wrote this biographical sketch, there were living aged people who remembered when he lived in Willimantic and kept his inn in that village. At what time he left Windham is not known, but probably about the year 1800. It is said he first went to join his father-in-law, Col. Eleazer Fitch, who went from Windham some years before, and who had a large tract of land, granted to him by the British Government, near Lake Memphremagog. Of his history after leaving Windham little is known Though a man of fine talents and education, he did not accumulate wealth, which is not a remarkable event when we look over the history of our most noted scientific men. Mr. Weaver says: "We have seen a letter written by him dated January 20, 1820." "He was then sixty-eight years old and living at Cochecton, Sullivan County, New York, where he died. He was then engaged in the lumber business. He speaks of breaking his arm by slipping on the ice on the Delaware river. He speaks of his children, Henry and Bela, whom he wishes to hear from, and also of his daughter, Annie, who, it seems, was with him. The letter is an interesting one, showing a right state of feeling in regard to his family, and expressing thankfulness for blessings received."

Bela Elderkin was a large, fine looking man, full six feet high and well proportioned. In fact, the Windham Elderkins were a noble race of men physically. The wife of Bela Elderkin, we judge, was also a large person. Col. Fitch, her father, was the largest and finest looking man in Windham, being six feet four inches in height and weighing over 300 pounds. It is not to be wondered at that some of their descendants were of gigantic proportions.

Bela Elderkin married Philena Fitch March 18, 1773.

She died December 8, 1796.

He died at Cochecton, Sullivan County, New York, (date unknown.)

THEIR CHILDREN—SIXTH GENERATION.

1. Jedediah, born January 1, 1774, went into Maine and engaged in the lumber business.

2. Eleazer, born June 28, 1775, was commander of a vessel that sailed out of Providence for many years, sometime in the employ of the late Cyrus Butler, and afterwards as owner. He married — first, a Miss

Sabin, of Providence, Rhode Island, who died, leaving no child; he married—second, a Miss Davis, a niece of the late Cyrus Butler. He is spoken of as a fine man, who accumulated some property. They died many years since in Providence, leaving one daughter, who is married and lived in New Bedford, Mass.

3. Thomas Mason Fitch Elderkin, born October 5, 1778, married Polly Buck, of Windham, August 27, 1797; had one son, George, born November 14, 1798. She died September 13, 1799, aged twenty-one; he died at Windham, 1808. It is said he was a hatter by trade.

4. Henry Elderkin, born August 2, 1780. It is said he was in the British naval service in the War of 1812.

5. Bela Elderkin, Jr., born September 30, 1782, died in Demerara, according to the Windham "Herald" of September, 1801, though, if such was the fact, it is singular that his father should not have known about it in 1820.

6. George Elderkin, born November 2, 1784, was a nail cutter by trade, and was, we judge, rather a wild boy. He left Windham early, and we have no further account of him.

7. Anthony Yeldat Elderkin, born Dec. 9, 1786.

8. Annie Elderkin, born Nov. 1789, married a Mr. Pond and lived in Franklin, Mass.

9. Mira Elderkin, born Jan. 19, 1793, married and lived in New Bedford, Mass. We have no further knowledge of the descendants of Bela Elderkin except through his seventh son, Anthony Y.

Anthony Yeldat Elderkin was born in the village of Willimantic, Dec. 9, 1786. His mother dying when he was about ten years old, he was placed in the family of Jabez Fitch, says a descendant of the latter, where he remained some years, probably until he left Windham. He went to Middlebury, Vt., at the age of 18, where he learned the wheelwright trade. In 1808 he removed to Potsdam, St. Lawrence County, N. Y., where he continued to reside until his death. He was a very large, tall and fine looking man, being 6 feet 7 inches high, well proportioned and weighed 320 pounds. He was highly esteemed in all the relations of life. Says a correspondent, "He was a good citizen and a kind father, a strong democrat, an Episcopalian and a mason." He married at Middlebury Vt., Parmela Fuller, daughter of Capt Josiah, Jan. 20, 1807; he died in 1831, aged 45; she died at Lancaster, Wis., since 1860.

THEIR CHILDREN—SEVENTH GENERATION.

NAMES.	BORN.	MARRIED TO.	DATE OF MAR.	DIED.
1. Elmina L.	Nov. 7, 1807.	Velonis Freeman.		Aug. 1881.
2. An infant.	July 11, 1809.			Aug. 28, 1809.
3. Noble Strong	Aug. 28, 1810.	1. Eliza Holden. 2. Mrs. Fanny (Cl'k) Putnam.	Dec. 29, 1835.	Dec. 29, 1875.
4. Mira.	Sept. 20, 1812.	Herman B. Fisher.	1832	
5. Edward.	Jan. 5, 1815.	Mary M. Beardsly.	1843.	Dec. 11, 1887.
6. William	Nov. 17, 1816.			July 20, 1833.
7. Catherine.	Oct. 27, 1818.			Aug. 5, 1819.
8. Martha.	July 19, 1822.	Harrison H. Hyde.		
9. Harriet	Dec. 21, 1824.	A. M. Sanford.		
10. Horace J.	Nov. 13, 1826.			Oct. 23, 1827.
11. An infant.	Aug. 16, 1829.			Oct 21, 1829.

Velonis Freeman, born

Elmina Elderkin, born Nov. 7, 1807.

Married.

THEIR CHILDREN—EIGHTH GENERATION.

1. Edward Anthony Freeman, born June 21, 1843.

Mrs. Elmina L. Freeman died Aug. 3, 1880, leaving one son, Edward A. Freeman, who is located at Canton, St. Lawrence County, N. Y.

Edward A. Freeman, married Maria Chamberlain of Madrid, N. Y They have one little daughter. Velonis Freeman was a farmer. He died May 8 or 9, 1883. His son still lives on the old farm.

Mrs. Elmina Freeman was the eldest child of Anthony Y. Elderkin. She was a very kind person to the poor, an affectionate wife and mother, and very proud of her Elderkin ancestry.

Hon Noble Strong, born Aug. 28, 1810.

1st married Eliza Holden, who died April 8, 1850.

2d married Mrs. Fanny (Clark) Putnam, May 18, 1851.

(Address, Potsdam, St. Lawrence County, N. Y.)

CHILDREN BY FIRST WIFE—EIGHTH GENERATION.

NAMES.	BORN.	MARRIED TO.	DATE OF MAR.	DIED.
1. W. Anthony	May 15, 1839.	Fanny Gurley.	June, 1861.	
2. Sarah L.	Dec. 17, 1841.			April 5, 1847.
3. Frances E.	Aug. 6, 1844.	Horace Smith.		May 5, 1868.
4. N. Edward.	Sept. 7, 1847.			April 30, 1848.
5. Emma L.	Jan. 21, 1850.			April 17, 1850.
		By second wife.		
6. N. Strong, Jr.	July 24, 1852.	Lena Wicker.		

Hon. Noble S. Elderkin, eldest son of Anthony Y., was born at Potsdam, St. Lawrence County, N Y., where he received such educational advantages as the common school and academy of his native town afforded. For several years he taught school winters and worked in his father's wheelwright shop summers. He was first elected constable of Potsdam, then appointed deputy sheriff, acting in that capacity for several years, until 1843, when he was elected high sheriff of St Lawrence County for three years. In this office he discharged its duties with unflinching courage and ability. He was elected a member of the Legislature of the State of New York, from St. Lawrence County three years in succession, to wit: 1849, 1850, and 1851. During his second term he was Speaker in the Assembly or House of Representatives. At some time he became acquainted with Wm. L. Weaver, of Windham, Ct., who had made extensive researches after the history of the first settlers of his native town. From him Mr. Elderkin procured all the early history of the Elderkin family. He was also a friend to the State Malitia, and filled all the important grades of military offices in the same up to, and including the rank of, Brigadier General. He was 6 feet high and weighed 200 lbs., and was a Silas Wright Democrat. I am not informed as to his religious faith, but can see clearly that he acted well his part in life, which is the essence of all goodness. He died Dec. 29, 1875, being 65y. 3m. 1d. old.

Miss Eliza Holden, first wife of Noble S., was the daughter of Capt. Jonas Holden, of Potsdam. She was the mother of five children; was married Dec. 29, 1835, and died April 8, 1850.

Miss Fannie Clark first married Rev. A. K. Putnam, rector of Trinity Church of Potsdam. For her second husband, Noble S. Elderkin, by whom she was the mother of one son, Noble Strong, Jr. She is a lady of refinement, intelligence and liberality; devoted to progress and reform in all the movements that add to the wisdom, goodness and happiness of mankind. She is yet living at the old homestead at Potsdam, St. Lawrence County, N. Y—The compiler of this work must express his gratitude and many thanks to Mrs. Fannie Elderkin for the early history of our family, also to her scribe, Edith S. Wilcox, who, from the old musty records and papers of the past, brought forward, with so much ability and order, the life shadows of an ancestry who have long rested from the conflicts of this world, yet still speak and act in the persons of a numerous offspring, who, in their stead, are now laboring in love for humanity's sake. Mrs. Elderkin was born March 11, 1819

(Address, Newport Barracks, Kentucky.)

Major William Anthony Elderkin was born May 15, 1839, at Potsdam, N. Y. He entered the U. S. military academy at West Point, July :, 1856; graduated May 6, 1861, and received a commission as second lieutenant in the 1st regiment, U. S. Artillery. He served during the Rebellion from 1861 to 1866; in the defenses of Washington, D. C from May to July, 1861, in the Manassas campaign of 1861, being engaged in the battle of Bull Run, July 21, 1861, as junior officer of Ricketts Light Battery—afterwards on duty in the defenses of Washington until Sept., 1861, when he was promoted to 1st lieutenant May 14, 1861. He was on duty with Battery H, 1st artillery in Hooker's division on the Lower Potomac until Jan. 1862, when he was ordered to duty as assistant professor of mathematics and instructor of artillery tactics at the U. S. Military Academy at West Point. There he remained on that duty until Aug., 1864; then received appointment, July 4, 1864, Capt. of staff, Commissary of Subsistence. On temporary duty with Depot Commissary at Washington, D. C, to Oct. 15, 1864. He was Depot Commissary at Louisville, Ky., from Oct. 15, 1864, to July 22, 1865. March 13, 1865, he was appointed Major by Brevet, for faithful and meritorious services during the Rebellion. He was ordered to Mobile, Ala., Aug. 1865, where he was Chief Commissary of the Department of Alabama to Dec., 1865; purchasing and depot Commissary at same place up to Jan. 23, 1867; Chief Commissary, district of the Chattahoochee to Feb. 19, 1867, and of the district of Georgia and Alabama to April 11, 1867. He was chief Commissary of the first military district of Richmond, Va., from April 24, 1867, to June, 1869; Sheriff of the city of Richmond, by military appointment, from March to June, 1869. He was supervising Commissary for Indians in the department of the Missouri from July, 1869, to July, 1870; depot commissary at Ft. Lyon, Col., from July to October, 1870; depot and purchasing Commissary at Denver, Col, to May, 1872, at Pueblo, Col., to March,

1876, at Ft. Leavenworth, Kan., from April, 1, 1876, to April 9, 1877. Purchasing and depot Commissary at Sioux City, Iowa, to April, 1878, at Yankton, Dakota, to September, 1880, and at Cheyenne, Wyoming Territory, from October, 1880, to January, 1881; chief Commissary department of Arkansas, at Little Rock, from February to May, 1881. He was purchasing and depot Commissary at Cheyenne, Wyoming Territory, from June, 1881, to July, 1882. At this date he obtained leave of absence to March, 1883. His period of continued service extending from 1861 up to 1882, twenty-one years. This was a long time of constant labor and care without a jubilee.

He returned to his duties as Chief Commissary of the department of the Columbia, at Vancovers Barracks, April, 1883, where he remained until November, 1884. In December, 1884, he was located as Purchasing and Department Commissary at Newport Barracks, Cincinnati, O., where he remained at last account, May 4, 1885.

We have been minute in recording the biography of Major William Anthony Elderkin because he is now in the vigor of manhood and on the active stage of life as one of the guardians of the people's liberty. In his abilities the nation, as well as every individual, has an interest. His ability, integrity, honesty and manhood have been thoroughly tested, and proved to be without fault so far as is known to the writer.

Major William Anthony Elderkin is an officer of fine personal appearance and noble, manly bearing. His height is 5 feet 11 inches, weight about 200 pounds, with brown hair and blue eyes, bringing down to the eighth generation the same personal characteristics of his ancestors. We believe his future greatness and notoriety will only depend upon a great emergency that might call him to act in a higher sphere of command.

Major William A Elderkin was born May 15, 1839.

Miss Fannie Gurley was born July 6, 1841.

They were married June 9, 1861.

THEIR CHILDREN—NINTH GENERATION.

NAMES.	BORN.	MARRIED TO.	DATE OF MAR.	DIED.
1 Anna McNair	May 21, 1862.			
2 Evie Kingsbury.	Aug. 14, 1863.	Geo. F. Wilson.	Nov. 20, 1884.	
3 Wm. Schuyler	1867.			1867.
4 Eliza Gurley.	Jan. 9, 1869.			
5 Chas. Stanton	Dec. 1870.			June, 1876.
6 Phineas Gurley.	Dec. 1872.			May, 1876.

Mrs. Fannie G. Elderkin is the daughter of Rev. R. R. Gurley, of Washington, D. C. Miss Evie Kingsbury Elderkin married George F. Wilson, assistant surgeon, United States army.

Miss Frances Eliza Elderkin, born Aug. 6, 1844.

Horace Smith, born

(Address Canton, St. Lawrence Co., N. Y.)

They were married

They had one son (ninth generation) William Elderkin Smith, who resided with his father at Canton.

Mrs. Frances E. Smith died May 5, 1868.

Noble Strong Elderkin, Jr., born July 24, 1852.

Lena S. Wicker, born April 21, 1856.

They were married Oct. 11, 1876.

(Address, 235 Wabash avenue, Chicago, Ill.)

THEIR CHILDREN—NINTH GENERATION.

1. Noble Strong, 3rd born Jan. 2, 1878.

2. George W. Elderkin, born Oct. 5, 1879.

Noble S. Elderkin, Jr., is the youngest son of Hon. Noble S. Elderkin by his second wife. He was born at Potsdam, St. Lawrence Co., N. Y., where he received an excellent English education and a thorough training in the elements of a business life. Following the current of imigration, he removed to Woodstock, Ill., previous to Oct. 11, 1876, where he found and married his wife, who was born and educated in that town. His business capacity, honesty and veracity are clearly attested by the fact that he has been in the employ of the Singer Sewing Machine Manufacturing Company fourteen years, giving complete satisfaction to the company. About four years of that time he spent at the Quincy, Indianapolis and St. Louis branches of the same firm. The remaining ten years he has been with the Chicago house.

His height is 6 feet, weight 154 pounds. His hand-writing is entirely foreign to the Elderkin style, which is remarkably uniform through several generations. Noble S. Elderkin's hand-writing indicates activity, energy and uniformity of habits. In work or business he dashes ahead like a locomotive, clearing the track before him and whirling forward the burden behind him. In cases of emergency he has often discharged the duties of two hands at the same time. His industry, energy and economy have built up for him a fine house with pleasant surroundings, in the north part of Chicago, near Lincoln Park, where he now resides.

Mira Elderkin, born Sept. 20, 1812,

Herman B. Fisher, born Nov. 18, 1805.

They were married Feb. 27, 1831.

(Address, Lancaster, Wis.)

THEIR CHILDREN—EIGHTH GENERATION.

NAMES.	BORN.	MARRIED TO.	DATE OF MAR.	DIED
1. Edward E.	Oct. 5, 1834.			Jan. 25, 1842.
2. Hiram S.	Nov. 11, 1836.			Feb. 28, 1851.
3. Harriet P.	Sept. 13, 1838.			
4. Hewlett W.	April 3, 1846.			
5. Edith P.	April 29, 1856.			

Mr. Herman B. Fisher is a mason by trade, but after he moved West he became a farmer. The family were sick at the time I wrote for information, which accounts for the defect in the description of their family. Their son Hewlett W. lives in Boston. One of their daughters is married to Jared Barnet. They live in Lancaster, Wis., and have seven children.

Hon. Edward Elderkin, attorney and counselor at law, was born at Potsdam, Jan. 5, 1815.

(Address, 1036 Pearl street, Racine, Wis.)

The following biographical sketch of himself, wife and family, though short, cannot fail to attract the attention and awaken an interest in the mind of every relative, however remote the relationship. His scholarship is extensive; his integrity unbending; his philanthropy and generosity unlimited. Though feeble in youth he has passed his 71st year and still lives to bless mankind with his good counsel and example. What we have of his history is authentic, being written by himself

A genealogical sketch of Edward Elderkin, fifth child and third son of Anthony Y. and Pamela Fuller Elderkin and of his children, written out April 6, 1885, at Racine, Wis:

" Edward had the opportunities of a common school in his native village of Potsdam, St. Lawrence County, State of New York, where he was born, Jan. 5, 1815, and was the fifth child and third son of Anthony Y. and Pamela Fuller

Elderkin. At the age of 10 he was transferred to the lower department of St. Lawrence Academy which had recently been established in that village, where for one year he pursued the ordinary English studies, after which he entered into a larger class of young men who were fitting themselves for college Latin and Greek then became his studies in which for the first year he made slow progress, but in the second, third and fourth years, he, by constant application and hard study, succeeded in keeping up with the class, and the story of Virgil and the orations of Cicero and Homer's Iliad so enchanted him that he was said to excel in the dead languages. At this time, in the spring of 1830, he formed a resolution of entering college at Middleburg, Vt., in the fall of that year. But alas! How changeable are all human calculations! His father was suddenly taken away by death and was buried on Christmas day in 1830. His death changed all the plans Edward had formed and he was compelled at this youthful age to engage in school teaching to assist the older children to take up an incumbrance on the homestead and save a home for his mother. His father, previous to his death, had become involved in a large indebtedness by lending his name to a neighbor for $2 000, and this his children worked out after his death, occupying three years of time. This was a hard beginning for the young man who was assisted by an elder brother and two older sisters. The objective point, however, was at last reached, and mother, with her younger children, had a home free and clear from debt. In the fall of 1833, Edward entered the law office of Hon. Silas Wright, then a leading lawyer in the County of St. Lawrence, and since in the State and nation, and remained with him one year. Mr. Wright at this time, having been appointed to a state office at Albany, N. Y., kindly introduced his students to Hon. John Fine, of Ogdensburg, into whose office he entered to pursue his law studies. Judge Fine having a brother three miles from town, a retired gentleman farmer, located on the banks of the majestic St. Lawrence river, with a family of five children, wanting a teacher in his family, the subject of this sketch accepted his offer of $40 per month and taught his children for four years, still pursuing his law studies with the Judge, (this being a part of the contract). In August, 1838, Edward was examined at Utica, N. Y., in a class of 76 applicants and took his parchments as an Attorney and Counselor in the Supreme Court of the State. He was the next week also examined in chancery practice before the Hon. R. H. Walworth, the then Chancellor of the State, and took his diploma there also, this being considered a great victory, as at Albany out of 75 applicants 42 were deemed unworthy, not qualified, and some rejected by the courts. After reaching home and a rest of two weeks, Edward (having, while in Albany on his way home purchased a small library of law books) immediately opened an office in his native village where he continued in successful practice until October, 1839, when, his health failing him from over-work, and being advised by his physician to seek a new climate, he packed his books and a small stock of worldly goods and took stage for Ogdenburg in time to take the steamer up the St. Lawrence river on his way to the then unexplored, great Northwest Territory. He left home on the 13th of October and on the 25th of the same month, 1837, he reached Elk Horn, Walworth Co., Wis., landing among strangers, friendless and alone, with a brave heart and a persevering will to succeed. Elk Horn was, at this time, a small hamlet, 45 miles southwest of Milwaukee, then, as now, the metropolis of Wisconsin, and 40 miles due-west from Racine, his present place of residence. He found but four settlers at Elk Horn, but it was the County Seat and located in the midst of a lonely country of prairie and oak openings. Here he was kindly received and was pursuaded to stay, opening an office the next day after his arrival, being the second Attorney-at-Law in the county.

Here he married his wife, raised his children, had a good practice, was successful in his cases, never selling a cliant, (as is often the case) but adhering to the rule of "honest dealing with all," and thus securing a good and lucrative practice. In a few years he purchased a tract of land adjoining the village, of 450 acres and divided his time in later years between the law and toiling the soil. In 1849 his father-in-law and mother-in-law both died, leaving children, eight in number, and it became necessary, for their protection, care and education, to remove them to his home in Elk Horn, a distance of 30 miles. This family consisted of one full sister to his wife and seven of the half blood—three boys and four girls—the youngest two years old and ranging up to fourteen years This family found protection and care under his roof until maturity, and the girls went to California at an early day and died ; the boys gave their lives to their country in the War of the Rebellion. His children, except Susie, (Mrs. Dr. Wilcox) are all living, while the orphans, save one, are all dead. What a commentary on the mutability of human affairs. He continued his residence at Elk Horn until the fall of 1883, when from paralysis of his own body and the blindness of his wife it became necessary to change his location, and in November, 1883, he removed to Racine and here he is enjoying the companionship of three of his children and one grandchild (Susie), whose interests are confided to the care of her aunt Emma, his eldest child. In concluding the sketch of this scion of one of the Elderkin families of America, it may be not improper to add that Edward, from ten years old to the present time, has pulled the laboring oar, and in a more familiar phrase, "has paddled his own canoe," and being surrounded by his stricken wife, his eldest child, Emma, who has the care of the household, and above all his granddaughter Frankie Elderkin Wilcox who is a care and yet is considered by him and his family as a great pleasure and the light and life of the household. Long may the Elderkin race flourish and be found doing good deeds and having friends with the whole world, reach a happy ending.

Edward Elderkin and Mary Martha Beardsley were married at Elk Horn, Wisconsin, on Christmas eve, December 24th, 1843, by the Rev. J. Lloyd Breck, Episcopal

Mary M. Beardsley was born at Walton, Delaware Co., N. J, Nov. 27th, 1816.

CHILDREN.

1. Emma Pamila Elderkin was born at Elk Horn, Wisconsin, November 23d, 1844.

2. Adelaide Elderkin (Mrs. W. A. Brown) was born July 31st, 1846.

3. Edward Anthony Elderkin was born July 3d, 1848.

4. Noble Henry Elderkin was born March 22d, 1850.

5. Frank Bennett Elderkin was born October 4th, 1852.

6 Susie Gardiner Elderkin was born August 14th, 1854.

7. Harriet Elderkin (Mrs. Frank Pardee) was born November 23d, 1856.

Average weight of the boys, 150 ; girls, 130. Eyes blue, hair light brown, and all free from any inherited disease.

Miss Emma Pamelia Elderkin, eldest child of Hon. Edward Elderkin, Esq , and his wife, Mary Martha, was born at Elk Horn, Wisconsin, November 23d, 1844. Present address, 1036 Pearl St , Racine, Wisconsin. She remains unmarried and resides with her parents conducting the household affairs and kindly sustaining her feeble father and mother in their declining years. She is the guardian of little Frankie Elderkin Wilcox, who is a brilliant little girl about eight years old Her aunt is very kind to her and takes great interest in her progress at school.

Adelaide Elderkin was born July 31st, 1846. She married William A. Brown at Elk Horn, February 7th, 1870.

His business I have not been able to learn.

(Address, Racine Wisconsin.)

THEIR CHILDREN—NINTH GENERATION.

1. Mary Emma, born December 2d 1873, died September 2d, 1877.

2. (Name not given.)

Edward Anthony Elderkin, born July 3d, 1848.

Laura Alice Glass, born May 19th, 1853.

(Address, Racine, Wisconsin.)

They were married January 20th, 1876.

His occupation is not reported. She is the daughter of Homer and Laura Glass.

THEIR CHILDREN—NINTH GENERATION.

1. Louis Elmer, born November 5th, 1877.

2. Lillian Beardsley, born February 23d, 1882.

Noble Henry Elderkin, born March 22d, 1850. Address, Elk Horn, Wisconsin. He is a printer by trade, and sticks to the old homestead and his old office at Elk Horn. He is a man of education, ability and stability of character.

Frank Bennett Elderkin. born at Elk Horn, Wisconsin, October 4th, 1852.

Emma S. Garretson was born at Winterset, Iowa, October 26th, 1862.

They were married at Winterset, April 17th, 1880.

(Address, Winterset, Iowa.)

His height is 5 ft. 4 inches; weight 150 lbs. Her height is 5 ft. 4½ inches; weight 135 lbs

Frank B. Elderkin graduated from the high school of Elk Horn in 1873 at the age of 21 years, when he engaged in the dray business for a period of six years. He removed to Winterset, Iowa, March 1st, 1878; became a clothier in 1880, at which trade he is still employed. His business is prosperous and he is a highly respected citizen.

Emma S., his wife, was born at Winterset, Iowa where she received a common school education. Her father, N. W. Garretson, was born in Indiana, emigrated to Winterset, Iowa, in 1851, owned and conducted a large harness store at that place for several years. He removed to Portland, Oregon, in 1874. She returned to Winterset in 1880. Her father is evidently a man of talent, ability and courage. He presided as Judge of the court of Madison County for two terms. Was chief agent for the North western Insurance Company for several years. At one time he resided in Washington Territory, and if yet alive is supposed to be at his old home in Winterset, Iowa.

CHILDREN OF FRANK B. AND EMMA S. ELDERKIN. NINTH GENERATION.

1. Archie Lysle, born at Winterset, July 17th, 1881.

2. Glenn Pardee, born at Winterset, December 17th, 1883.

This family are all light complexion, light hair and blue eyes, which are characteristics of the race of Elder ins.

Susie Gardiner Elderkin, born August 14th, 1854.

Emmons T. Wilcox, M. D., born February 13th, 1852.

They were married October 25th, 1875, by Rev. Charles M. Pullen, Recto1 of St. John's Church Susie died at Garrison, Iowa. April 4th, 1884, and was buried on the 16th at Racine, Wisconsin, from her father's house, Rev. Mr. Gold Episcopal, officiating. She was a dearly beloved daughter, sister, wife and mother.

Dr. Emmons T. Wilcox is the son of a Methodist Clergyman, born at Canaan, Pennsylvania. In July, 1855, his parents removed to Wisconsin. He commenced the study of medicine under G. H. Young, M. D., in 1873, graduated with the class honors at Keokuk College of Physicians and Surgeons, February, 1876. He entered practice as a partner of Dr. Saunders, at Thompson, Ill., removed to Wisconsin in January, 1877 at Washburn, where he practiced until 1880, when he attended lectures and graduated at Mro. Department, University of New York. Thence he returned to Wisconsin until 1882 when he went to Chicago for special courses of study and formed a partnership with Prof. H. C. Cotton. He afterwards returned to Garrison, Iowa, where he remained until after the death of his wife, 1884. The writer is informed that he is a man of elevated ambition, thoroughly educated in his profession, a successful practitioner, and a standard man in all the good qualities that make up manhood.

THEIR CHILDREN—NINTH GENERATION.

Frankie Elderkin Wilcox, born October 17th, 1877, at Washburn, Grant County, Wisconsin.

Harriet Elderkin, born November 23d, 1856.

Frank Pardee, born December 25th, 1851.

They were married May 23d, 1877.

(Address, East Grove, Ill.)

Hattie Pardee is so little and handsome and kind, refined and good, that everybody loves her. Her hand writing is a fac simile of the Elderkin style. She seems to this old third cousin like one of his own daughters. She has the light complexion and hair, and blue eyes of the race, but is done up in most too small a package to compare with her ancestors, weighing only 106 pounds. Her husband weighs only 109 pounds. No wonder they are *good*; if they were not there would be nothing of them. But, it is said, "costly material must be done up in small packages."

THEIR CHILDREN—NINTH GENERATION.

1. Frank Wilcox Pardee, born March 17th, 1878.
2. Mary Elizabeth Pardee, born October 4th, 1883.

The family of Hon. Edward Elderkin, Esq., are all well brought up, educated, refined and good citizens and useful members of society.

Martha P. Elderkin, daughter of Anthony Y. Elderkin, and Parmela Fuller Elderkin, was born July 19th, 1822.

(Address, Lancaster, Grant County, Wisconsin.)

Harrison H. Hyde, born June 11th, 1818.

Mr. Hyde died in Lancaster, March 16th, 1864.

Mrs. Martha P. Hyde was married September 20th, 1843. Her life has been checked with sadness and sunshine. At the tender age of 8 years her father died, cutting off that parental guardianship so essential to youth. She was sent to school to qualify herself for teaching, and at the early age of 15 taught her first school of five months at one dollar per week. She was located 30 miles from home and did not visit her mother during the term. For one so young, that time must have seemed an age. Deer River, a branch of the St. Lawrence, divided the district, and the bridge was carried away by a flood that spring, so she learned to row a boat in which she crossed the stream two or three times a day. Thus she learned, literally, to paddle her own canoe.

Her husband was a dentist by trade, and possessed remarkable mechanical talent. He made some of his best dental instruments and at one time made a very beautiful double-barreled rifle. He was 5 ft. 11 inches in height and weighed 164 pounds Mr. Hyde was a kind and affectionate husband and father, an excellent tenor singer and very highly esteemed by the community in which he lived.

During their married life of 21 years Martha collected all the sunshine and flowers that a cheerful, hopeful keen perception could discover in a world of such strange mutations. She was left with a family or five small children to care for with only a small fortune to rely upon. She lost a twin son only a few days after her husband's death. The change was great, the shock crashing; but she rallied, applied the oars of endurance and perserverance and has for the last 21 years again paddled her own canoe. In attempting to give us a sketch of her life she broke down over the magnitude of the retrospective view and appealed to her son Charles, a gentleman and scholar, to write for her. He says:

"I speak, as a son, concerning the best mother on earth. Her experience can hardly be related—it must be felt by those who have had a similar experience. She has borne her countless misfortunes with never-ending patience. The care and tenderness and watchfulness that she manifested when Eddie (my youngest brother suffered so long with a 'white swelling" could be only displayed by a mother. Mothers! The bulk of human patience endurance, love and care, belong to them"

In her children. whose hearts are overflowing with gratitude, she finds a great reward for all her cares. Martha P. Hyde is a fine looking woman; height 5 ft. 7 inches, weight 120 pounds.

THEIR CHILDREN—EIGHTH GENERATION.

NAMES.	BORN.	MARRIED TO.	DATE OF MAR.	DIED.
1. Hattie E.	Oct. 5, 1847.			June 25, 1848.
2. Helen A.	Nov. 29, 1849.	Chas. A. Cox.		
3. George B.	Sept. 19, 1851.	Alice Green.	Feb. 24, 1874.	
4. Charles S.	Feb. 21, 1861.			
5. Edward H.	Jan. 25, 1863.			
6. Freddie H.	Jan. 25, 1863.			April 8, 1864.

Helen A. Hyde, born Nov. 29th, 1849.
Charles A. Cox, born ———
They were married ———
(Address, Lancaster, Grant County, Wisconsin)

Mr. Cox is a farmer and lives about four miles from Lancaster. His personal qualities are not reported, nor those of his wife. Her height is 5 ft. 4 inches ; weight 137 pounds They have four children.

George B. Hyde, born September 19th, 1851.
Alice Green, born ———
Married February 24th, 1874.
(Address, Lancaster, Grant County. Wisconsin.)

Mr. Hyde is a machinist by trade, an excellent workman and resides in Lancaster. His wife resided at Indianapolis before his marriage. They have three children. His height is 5 ft. 10 inches ; weight 164 pounds.

Charles S. Hyde, born in Lancaster, February 21st, 1861.
(Address, Lancaster, Grant County, Wisconsin.)

His height is about 6 ft., weight 160 pounds.

He is finely educated and an excellent teacher, being now employed as a principal of a graded school at Groyling, Michigan. He attended a popular school in the State of Indiana. His wages at the present time are $75 per month. He partakes largely of the Elderkin blood and characteristics, is true hearted, strongly attached to home and friends, honest, energetic and intellectual. His desire for scientific knowledge is large and unsatisfied. The present tendencies of his mind, if he is permitted to live to old age, will certainly make him a useful man in society.

Harriet Gray Elderkin, daughter of Anthony Y., and Parmela Elderkin, was born at Pottsdam, December 21st, 1824.
Aulelus M. Sanford, born May 28th, 1812.
They were married December 29th, 1850.
(Address, 3156 State St., Chicago, Illinois.)

Mr Sanford is a man of business tact, and though now

74 years old, is actively engaged in one of the offices of the Singer Sewing Machine Company, of Chicago.

THEIR CHILDREN—NINTH GENERATION.

1. Lillie C. Sanford, born December 12th, 1858.

2. Charles Elderkin Sanford, born December 12th, 1863. Died May 30th, 1867.

CHAPTER XII.

Alfred Elderkin, Esq., youngest son of Col. Jedediah Elderkin, was born Jan. 4, 1759. He partially fitted for college, intending to enter Yale, but a long illness which lamed him for life prevented, and he remained at home, aiding his father in superintending his farm and factories. He was the executor of his father's will, and was engaged in various kinds of business in the latter part of his life. We are told that he was for a time in the jewelry business with his neighbor, Mr. Staniford. He was a tall and rather large man, and of course is well remembered by many people in Windham. He married Sarah Brown, daughter of Samuel and Sarah (Bishop) Brown, January 27, 1779. She died March 4, 1833; he died October 9, 1833, being 74 years 9 months and 5 days old. They lived in the red gambrel-roofed house, west of the Staniford tavern, now owned by Mr. George Lathrop.

THEIR CHILDREN—SIXTH GENERATION.

NAMES.	BORN.	MARRIED TO.	DATE OF MAR.	DIED.
1. Sally.	Aug. 8, 1779.	Jas. S. Campbell.		
2. Fanny.	Nov. 21, 1781.	1st. Cuthbert; 2d, Baker.		
3. Bishop.	Feb. 16, 1784.			Oct. 16, 1791.
4. Lora.	Feb. 20, 1786.			Jan., 1863.
5. Judith.	Aug. 2, 1788.			Jan. 1, 1811.

Of this family we have but one living branch, the children of Sally Campbell.

Fanny Elderkin was twice married, lived in West Hartford, Connecticut, where she died, leaving no child.

Bishop Elderkin, the only son, died at the age of seven years, thus obliterating the name of Elderkin from Alfred's descendants.

Lora Elderkin lived at Cherry Valley, N. Y., and died at the age of 77 years, unmarried.

Judith Elderkin died at the age of 21 years, unmarried.

Sally Elderkin, eldest child of Alfred Elderkin, was born August 8th, 1779. She married, on December 1, 1799, Jas. S. Campbell, of Cherry Valley, New York, where they spent a long life in health and happiness. On the 1st of December, 1864, they celebrated the sixty-fifth anniversary of their marriage, when six sons of the venerable couple were present. At last accounts they were enjoying comfortable health, Mr. Campbell at the age of 92 years, and Mrs. Campbell at the age of 86 years. The time of their deaths unknown.

THEIR CHILDREN—SEVENTH GENERATION.

1. Alfred E., D. D.,	residence,	New York.
2. Mary Ann,	"	Cherry Valley.
3. William W., LL. D.,	"	Cherry Valley.
4. Geo. W.,	"	Cherry Valley.
5. Samuel B.,	"	Castleton, N. Y.
6. James Henry,	"	New York.
7. John Cannon,	"	New York.
8. Augustus, M. D.,	"	Gloversville, N. Y.

They were all living in 1860. The family is a highly respected and talented one, and Judge William W. Campbell has been on the bench many years and has received the honorary degree of LL. D.

In 1865 Wm. L. Weaver published in the "Willimantic Journal" a sketch of the Elderkin family, so far as he had been able to trace them, from 1637 to 1865. At the close of his article he says: "We have been much interested in tracing this family. *It was of good stock*, and unlike some of our early families, *has not deteriorated.* Descendants in both the male and female lines are highly respectable, and many talented men are found among them. Some of the characteristics of the family are patriotism, ambition, a love of military life, frankness, liberality and public spirit."

To the above might be added with propriety, that as a race of people they are strictly honest, and with few exceptions they have all embraced the Christian religion. So far as the writer has been able to learn, not one of the Elderkin name has been convicted of a crime in the ten generations as recorded in this work, and only one case reported among the descendants on the female intermarriages.

Very few, if any, have possessed an inordinate desire to accumulate wealth, while most of them have procured a competency. The almost universal tendency to acquire a good education is worthy of note. The inclination in this direction appears to be hereditary, and we have no knowledge of a family so extensive where educated men and women were so numerous. The marriages as a rule have been remarkably good; the mental and moral organization lead them into families of like culture and affinities, proving the old adage, "birds of a feather will flock together." Wherever there has been a marriage by an individual into a lower stock of people, the children have suffered from the grade, but fortunately but few cases of this kind have occurred, and these mostly in the eighth and ninth generations.

Another old saying is, "blood tells," and any person whose mind has been directed toward the classes of the human family has seen that ancestors of a peculiar character will send that character down in their posterity for hundreds of years. When a young man, I knew a family near Jamestown, N. Y., who were petty thieves. In the progress of time I became acquainted with the several neighborhoods in a southwesterly direction for a distance of 54 miles. On this entire route I found low families of different names that would steal, and wonderful as it may seem, they were all relatives by intermarriage with the Jamestown family. The electric and mental affinities are just as strong, comparatively, between toads as between philosophers. There are three kinds of affinities: mental, moral and electric. Mental affinity is determined by the judgment after obtaining, by acquaintance, a knowledge of the qualities of mind of our associates. If their thoughts, aspirations, acquirements and conclusions are like ours, then we have a genial companion, whose mental affinity will continue to the end of life. The moral affinity naturally grows out of the mental, and will rarely diverge from it. Electric affinity is much less trustworthy and enduring; it relates principally to the sexes, and will not stand the test of old age — in fact, it often expires after a period of intimate relations, when the electric forces become equalized. At this juncture the two persons, becoming each positively electrified, repel each other, and if they are husband and wife, will quarrel and part, if not held together by the mental and moral affinities. From these facts we readily see the importance of early education on the subject of matrimonial affinities. A well educated class of people are less liable to be influenced by magnetic attraction than the uncultivated. There have been but few cases of divorce in the Elderkin history. This family or race of people, taken in connection with other families of like grade and qualities of mind, make up the great central power of this nation of freemen. They are America's strength in war and her resources in time of peace They sustain the Christian church, prop the pillars of state, demand a just legislation and an equal and uniform administration of the laws. None of *our* great men could ever be bought or induced to sacrifice principle for place and power; hence our name has not been trumpeted through the columns of the political press. Opposition to dishonesty in high places is a sure doom to retirement and seclusion. The love of right and moral justice are so deeply rooted in the heads and hearts of the Elderkin connections and descendants that they rush to the rescue of the oppressed without regard to policy or personal loss or gain.

In concluding this work, which has occupied much of my time for a period of over two years, I submit it to my kinsfolk, feeling that from lack of information I may not have given you as brilliant a description as your merits would justify. Many members of the connection have expressed a diffidence in speaking of their own good qualities. A few have been passed to avoid the monotony of the same description. If I have done any one injustice, it arises from a mistake of the head and not from malice of the heart. My purpose has been to say truthfully what I have said, omitting small failings to which humanity, in a general sense, is subjected.

YOUR PEDIGREE.

EXTRACTS FROM A DISCOURSE BY REV. DR. TALMAGE.

"Whose son art thou, thou young man?"—1 Samuel xvii., 58.

The longer I live the more I believe in blood—good blood, bad blood, proud blood, humble blood, honest blood, thieving blood, heroic blood, cowardly blood. The tendency may skip a generation or two, but it is sure to come out, as in a little child you sometimes see a similarity to a great-grandfather whose picture hangs on the wall. That the physical and mental and moral qualities are hereditable is patent to any one who keeps his eyes open. The similarity is so striking sometimes as to be amusing. Great families, regal or literary, are apt to have the characteristics all down through the generations, and what is more perceptible in such families may be seen on a smaller scale in all families. A thousand years have no power to obliterate the difference.

The large lip of the House of Austria is seen in all the generations, and is called the Hapsburg lip. The house of Stewart always means, in all generations, cruelty and bigotry and sensuality. Scottish blood means persistence, English blood means reverence for the ancient, Welsh blood means religiosity, Danish blood means fondness for the sea, Indian blood means roaming disposition, Roman blood means conquest.

The Jewish facility for accumulation you may trace clear back to Abraham, of whom the Bible says, "he was rich in silver and gold and cattle," and to Isaac and Jacob, who had the same characteristics. Some families are characterized by longevity, and they have a tenacity of life positively Methusela-ish. Others are characterized by Goliathan stature, and you can see it for one generation, two generations, five generations, in all the generations. Vigorous theology runs on in the line of the Alexanders. Tragedy runs on in the family of the Kembles. Literature runs on in the line of the Trollopes. Philanthropy runs on in the line of the Wilberforces. Statesmanship runs on in the line of the Adamses. Henry and Catherine of Navarre religious, all their families religious. The celebrated family of the Casini—all mathematicians. The celebrated family of the Medici—grandfather, son and Catharine—all remarkable for keen intellect. The celebrated family of Gustavus Adolphus—all warriors.

This law of heredity asserts itself without reference to social or political condition; for you sometimes find the ignoble in high place and the honorable in obscure place. A descendant of Edward I. a toll gatherer. A descendant of Edward III. a doorkeeper. A descendant of the Duke of Northumberland a trunkmaker. Some of the mightiest families of England are extinct, while some of those most honored in the peerage go back to an ancestry of hard knuckles and rough exterior. This law of heredity is entirely independent of social or political condition. Then you find avarice and jealousy and sensuality and fraud having full swing in some families. The violent temper of Frederick William is the inheritance of Frederick the Great. It is not a theory to be set forth by worldly philosophy only, but by divine authority. Do you not remember how the Bible speaks of "a chosen generation," of "the generation of the righteous," of "the generation of vipers," of an "untoward generation," of "a stubborn generation," of "the iniquity of the past visited upon the children unto the third and fourth generations." So that the text comes to-day with the force of a projectile hurled from mightiest catapult—"Whose son art thou, thou young man?"

THE NORTON FAMILY.

The Norton family, of Berlin, Hartford county, Conn., are a family of considerable notoriety, possessing business tact and the ability to accumulate wealth. They are connected to the Elderkin family by the marriage of Dr. Vine Elderkin, of Ashville, N. Y., to Nancy Norton.

Thomas Norton was born in England and emigrated to Guilford in 1639, two years later than John Elderkin I.

HIS CHILDREN—SECOND GENERATION.

1. Thomas Norton II. He lived in Saybrook; married Elizabeth Mason.
2. John Norton.

Four daughters, names unknown.

Thomas Norton II. and Elizabeth (Mason) Norton.

THEIR FIRST CHILD—THIRD GENERATION.

1. Thomas Norton III.

Thomas Norton III., of Saybrook, married Rebecca Neil. The invoice of his estate at his decease was dated February 26, 1727, and the valuation amounted to 903 pounds, 14 shillings and 6 pence. The portion received by his son Jedediah was 74 pounds, 17 shillings and 3 pence, which indicates that he had a large family of eight or ten children.

FOURTH GENERATION.

4th child. Jedediah Norton; born December 3, 1712.

Jedediah Norton, born in Saybrook, December 3, 1712. Eunice Cowls, of Meriden, first wife. In 1746 he married Achsah Norton, born June 10, 1721; died August 8, 1805. Jedediah died March 7, 1794.

He bought a farm in the southern part of Berlin, where he lived and died.

CHILDREN BY FIRST WIFE—FIFTH GENERATION.

1. Jedediah Norton II.
2. Eunice Norton.

CHILDREN BY SECOND WIFE.

3. Josiah Norton.
4. Lydia Norton; married Mr. Thompson.
5. Rebecca Norton; married Mr. Wright and died September, 1837, aged 84. Her son, Norton Wright, was born November 28, 1777. He married Betsey Norton June 27, 1820, and died March 8, 1855, aged 77.
6. Samuel Norton I.; died when a child.
7. Samuel Norton II.; born Sunday, September 30, 1759.
8. Ruth Norton; married Mr. Upson.

They also had one other child, who died in infancy.

Samuel Norton II.; born in Berlin, September 30, 1759. Phoebe Edwards; born February 19, 1770. They were married January 22, 1789. He died October 22, 1832; she died August 13, 1854.

THEIR CHILDREN—SIXTH GENERATION.

NAMES.	BORN.	MARRIED TO.	DATE OF MAR.	DIED
1. Edward.	Feb. 15, 1790.			Nov. 5, 1868.
2. Betsey.	Aug. 13, 1791.			Dec. 9, 1820.
3. Nancy.	Sept. 17, 1793.	Vine Elderkin, M.D.	Mar. 30, 1826.	Jan. 2, 1880.
4. Harriet.	April 27, 1796.			July 7, 1863.
5. Hiram.	Oct. 17, 1798.			Feb. 22, 1826.
6. Philip.	Mar. 2, 1801.			July 26, 1880.
7. Henry.	April 10, 1803.			——— 1885.
8. Samuel III	Sept. 7, 1806.			Oct. 7, 1826.
9. George.	Feb. 11, 1810.			Dec. 9, 1829.
10. William.	June 21, 1812.			Oct. 10. 1877.

Samuel Norton II. was a farmer and an extensive land owner. He was a superior financier. His estate, real and bank stock, at his death invoiced between eighty and one hundred thousand dollars. In his will he gave to one-half of his children twice the amount given to the other half. To his daughter, Nancy Elderkin, he gave $1,000 at the time of her marriage and $12,000 in bank stock at his decease. Three only of his children had heirs.

Nancy Norton; born in Berlin, September 17, 1793. Vine Elderkin; born in Genesee, N. Y., January 5, 1797. They were married March 30, 1826.

The records of this family will be found on page 44.

Harriet Norton; born in Berlin, April 27, 1796. Freedom Heart; born August 28, 1796. They were married November 8, 1824.

Mr. Heart had a former wife, by whom he had a family of children.

HIS CHILDREN—SEVENTH GENERATION.

1. Julia; born June 26, 1816; married H. W. Heart, January 28, 1841; died April 3, 1847.

2. William C.; born March 13, 1818; married Helen Danforth.

3. Sarah A.; born Feb. 5, 1820; married Orris B. Savage, September 24, 1845.

4. James; born April 17, 1821; died December 3, 1821.

Harriet (Norton) Heart was a highly educated and accomplished lady. Her manners were easy and her conversation entertaining. She was kind, noble and intellectual, and highly esteemed by all who knew her. She received from her father's estate $6,000. She had no children.

Philip Norton; born in Berlin, Ct., March 2, 1801. Elizabeth Newbery; born in Wethersfield, May 31, 1810. They were married March 28, 1835.

THEIR CHILDREN—SEVENTH GENERATION.

1. Samuel W.; born Feb. 16, 1836.
2. John; born March 18, 1838.
3. Henrietta; born August 1, 1840.
4. Alice; born April 3, 1843.
5. George; born May 24, 1847.
6. Elizabeth; born August 26, 1849.
7. Sarah; born January 21, 1852.

Philip Norton was a very energetic business man, and accumulated a large property. He died July 26, 1880, leaving a bright, well-to-do family of children and grandchildren. Their address is Berlin, Hartford county, Ct.

Henry Norton; born April 10, 1803. Adelia M. Atwood, born February 27, 1805. They were married May 22, 1825.

Second wife, Mary Angeline Tuttle; born May 3, 1825; married May 3, 1849.

(Address, Berlin, Hartford county, Ct.)

CHILDREN BY FIRST WIFE—SEVENTH GENERATION.

1. Elizabeth M.; born November 8, 1827; died April 1, 1829.
2. Jane; born August 28, 1829; died November 5, 1832.
3. Amanda; born May 12, 1831; died November 4, 1832.
4. Samuel; born November 3, 1832; died June 13, 1833.
5. Adelia M.; born August 14, 1834.
6. Henry H.; born October 23, 1840.

CHILDREN BY SECOND WIFE.

7. Mary A.; born February 28, 1850.
8. Jane Martha; born December 12, 1852.
9. Edward W.; born February 14, 1855; died February 21, 1855.
10. Albert E.; born March 27, 1856.
11. Ida; born May 27, 1858.
12. Nettie; born May 26, 1860.

Henry Norton was a stirring, active man, but lacked the financial ability common to the Norton family. He has a family of bright, intellectual children.

THE WALKER FAMILY.

The Walker family are connected to the Elderkin family by the marriage of Dyer W. Elderkin to Cornelia Walker, second daughter and fourth child of Thomas Dewey Walker and Amelia (Hays) Walker. As a race they are noted for their industry, business tact and number of children. James Walker was of Irish descent and was married in Connecticut to Sarah Shapley, a lady of Scotch ancestry. They removed to Chenango county, New York, where they raised a family. He was an officer in the army of the Revolution, and continued in the service until the glorious victory of American independence was won.

THEIR CHILDREN—SIXTH GENERATION.

1. Shapley; married to Lois ——.
2. Samuel; " Clarrie ——.
3. James; " Jane Paget.
4. John.
5. Sally; " Ward King.
6. Lydia; " James Lee.
7. Anna; " Thomas Tanner.
8. Polly; " Joseph Beckwith.
9. Thomas D. " Amelia Hays.

SHAPLEY WALKER'S CHILDREN—SEVENTH GENERATION.

1, Willard; 2, Scovel; 3, James; 4, Clara, unmarried; 5, Almira, married Hon. Judge Stacy; 6, a daughter whose name is unknown.

SAMUEL WALKER'S CHILDREN—SEVENTH GENERATION.

1, Nathaniel; 2, Dewey; 3, Edward; 4, Simeon; 5, Samuel; 6, Ransom; 7, Nelson; 8, Willard; 9, William; 10, Lorane; 11, Marioh; 12, Harriet; 13, Sally; 14, Clarinda; 15, 16 and 17, three daughters whose names are not known.

JAMES WALKER'S CHILDREN--SEVENTH GENERATION.

1, Nicholas; 2, James; 3, Willard; 4, Daniel; 5, William; 6, Jane; 7, Hannah; 8, Sarah; 9, Julia.

JOHN WALKER'S CHILDREN—SENENTH GENERATION.

1, Dewey; 2, Abigail, married Mr. Nash; 3, Sally, married Quinn Tappin; 4, Sylvenus.

Mr. Nash lived near Adrian, Michigan; had a family.

Mr. Tappin lived in Toledo, Ohio; had two children.

SALLY (WALKER) KING'S CHILDREN—SEVENTH GENERATION.

Sally Walker married Ward King.

Their family record will be found with the King family.

LYDIA (WALKER) LEE'S CHILDREN—SEVENTH GENERATION.

1, James; 2, Alphonzo; 3, Daniel; 4, Erastus; 5, William; and several others.

ANNA (WALKER) TANNER'S CHILDREN—SEVENTH GENERATION.

1. Ira located near Cherry Creek, Chautauqua county; had a family.

2. John married and located near Mayville, Chautauqua county, N. Y.; they had two children, a daughter and son.

3. Sally married Eda Weatherly, Esq., of Kiantom. He is a man of energy and strong bias. They raised a family of four sons and two daughters. Two of their sons are noted for their educational acquisitions and business talents.

4. James.

5. Lydia married Isaac Wilcox and located near Mayville, Chautauqua county, N. Y., where they raised three children, two sons and a daughter. One of their sons is an attorney-at-law, located at Titusville, Pa

6. Jemima married Ira Boynton, who is yet living, nearly 90 years old. He has only two grandchildren of his family living, a grandson and granddaughter, located near Riceville, Crawford county, Pa.

7. Nichols.

POLLY (WALKER) BECKWITH'S CHILDREN—SEVENTH GENERATION.

1. John Beckwith, M. D. A man of remarkable rhetorical talent. The writer recollects hearing John, when a young man, tell a story of a dog and a woodchuck, which aroused the sympathies of the listeners to such an extent that every eye was filled with tears.

2. Walker Beckwith, whose characteristics and history are unknown.

Thomas Dewey Walker was born in Chenango county, N. Y., July 24, 1795. Amelia Hays was born September 26, 1796. They were married June 9, 1817. He died April 8, 1852; she died June 22, 1866.

Thomas D. Walker possessed a large amount of energy and enterprise. In an early day he moved to Freehold, Warren county, Pa., where he engaged in clearing up a farm and making shingles, which were hauled and sold at Westfield, Chautauqua county. His older sons usually drove the teams and on their return brought back loads of groceries, flour and dry goods, which were sold to his poor neighbors for labor. In this manner he supplied, during the pinching winter of 1844, many families who were almost starved. So straitened were some of those early settlers at that time that they fed their children on bran bread and hay tea Mr. Walker was a very kind man, of even temper and enduring patience. His affection and good will toward his wife and children were so strong that no jar ever occurred between them, and his generosity extended almost without limit toward his neighbors, who sometimes, through envy, returned evil for good. Amelia, his wife, was such a mother in every good word and work as few children have been blessed with. The neatness of her household affairs was unsurpassed. Her refined and moral instructions were deeply imprinted in the minds and memory of her children. They were both members of the Baptist church. She was the daughter of Rev. Caleb Hays and Anna (Cook) Hays. He administered to a Baptist church in Chenango county, N. Y., during a long and useful life. During the progress of their married lives, Thomas and Amelia Walker embraced the Universal faith and doctrine, in which they reared their family. To this faith both parents and children adhered with unshaken confidence through life and in the trying ordeal of death. They were both born in Chenango county, N. Y., where I think all their children were born. Thomas and his youngest two children, Denzil D. and Mary E., died from typhoid fever and bad medication. Their remains rest in the family lot in the cemetery at Columbus, Warren county, Pa. Of their eight children, only one survives at this writing, 1886.

THEIR CHILDREN—SEVENTH GENERATION.

NAMES.	BORN.	MARRIED TO.	DATE OF MAR.	DIED.
1. Daniel H.	June 21, 1818.	1, Sophia Hawkins. 2, Mrs. Elsa Greene.	Sept. 8, 1843. 1866.	Aug. 7, 1884.
2. Rachel.	Sept. 30, 1819.	Horace Pardee.	Sept. 8, 1842.	Dec. 2, 1883.
3. William.	July 28, 1821.	Mary DeLong.	June 6, 1844.	
4. Cornelia.	July 17, 1823.	D. W. Elderkin.	Sept. 8, 1842.	June 27, 1854.
5. Augustin H.	Nov. 1, 1826.	1, C. R. Barker. 2, L. H. Freeman.	Feb. 22, 1849. Jan. 14, 1854.	Apr. 23, 1880.
6. Samantha.	April 29, 1830.			Oct. 2, 1847.
7. Denzil D.	Nov., 1833.			May 5, 1852.
8. Mary E.	Jan. 5, 1837.			June 8, 1832.

This family were bright intellectually, medium size, well formed and developed physically, with very fine features.

Daniel N. Walker, eldest son of Thomas D. Walker, was born in Chenango county, N. Y., June 21, 1818.

Sophia Hawkins, Chautauqua county, N. Y.

Married September 8, 1843.

Second marriage to Mrs. Elsa Greene, 1866.

Mrs. Sophia Walker died March 21, 1865.

D. N. Walker died August 7, 1884.

(Address of Mrs. Elsa Greene Walker, Youngsville, Warren county, Pa.)

CHILDREN BY FIRST WIFE—EIGHTH GENERATION.

NAMES.	BORN.	MARRIED TO.	DATE OF MAR.	DIED.
1. Emily J.	March 1, 1845.			1846.
2. Clarance.	Nov. 9, 1846.			1851.
3. Rosa.	Oct 8, 1848.	Chester O. Wright.		
4. Edmond D.	June 28, 1850.	Mary E. Bixler.	Mar. 1, 1877.	
5. James H.	April 16, 1853.	Nettie A. Hyde.	May 4, 1882.	
6. Arloa S.	Feb. 15, 1855.	Alex. Patterson.	Oct. 6, 1870.	
7. Jessee D.	October, 1857.			
8. Charles.	July 15, 1860.			Feb. 15, 1878.
9. Mary M.	May 23, 1862.	Wm. Ripley.	Aug. 4, 1880.	Jan. 15, 1882.
10. Harley.	Sept. 11, 1863.			

Daniel Walker was an industrious farmer, very liberal and kind to his family and to neighbors He owned his farm and furnished a good living for his large family, which was augmented by six or seven minor children of his second wife. Sophia was a kind, good woman, but did not possess so large an amount of tact in business and economy as Elsa. She considered the remote as well as the most contiguous wants, and made provision for both. Daniel's children were all born in Freehold, Warren county, Pa.

Rosa Walker, born October 8, 1848, married Chester O. Wright.

(Address, Columbus, Warren county, Pa.)

THEIR CHILDREN—NINTH GENERATION.

1. Cyrus Wright; born December 1, 1862.

2. Matta Wright; born April, 1868.

Chester O Wright is a large, fine looking man. He owns a farm and is a carpenter and joiner by trade. Rosa is a short, fat little chub, who makes the sun shine wherever she goes.

Edmond D. Walker; born June 28, 1850.
Mary E. Bixler; born June 6, 1852.
They were married March 1, 1877.
(Address, Bellville, Richland county, Ohio.)

THEIR CHILDREN—NINTH GENERATION.

1. Charley L. Walker; born July 14, 1878, at Bellville, Ohio.

Edmond D. Walker is getting along nicely for a young farmer. It is said Mrs. Walker is a good helper and the best kind of a partner.

James H. Walker; born April 16, 1853.
Nellie A. Hyde; born January 1, 1863.
They were married May 4, 1882.
(Address, Youngsville, Warren county, Pa.)

James is a good, honest, industrious, generous young man, and his wife knows it.

Arloa Sophia Walker; born February 15, 1855.
Alexander A. Patterson; born June 15, 1845.
They were married October 6, 1870.
(Address, Fredericktown, Knox county, Ohio.)

THEIR CHILDREN—NINTH GENERATION.

1. George W. Patterson ; born August 14, 1871.
2. Frank C. Patterson ; born July 24, 1877.

Alexander A. Patterson is a merchant and postmaster. He was employed several years as a ticket agent in railroad office. Arloa is a charming, sprightly little woman.

Rachel Walker was born in the town of Green, Chenango county, N. Y., September 13, 1819.

Horace Pardee was born in Russia, Herkimer county, N. Y., November 10, 1820.

They were married September 8, 1842.

(Address, Lodi, Barber county, Kansas.)

Rachel Pardee died December 2, 1883.

THEIR CHILDREN—EIGHTH GENERATION.

NAMES.	BORN.	MARRIED TO.	DATE OF MAR.	DIED.
1. Amelia D.	Nov. 5, 1843.	1, George Ellis. 2, C. E. McQueen.	Mar. 31, 1862. Nov. 20, 1866.	
2. Averry C.	May 10, 1846.			May 10, 1846.
3. Adelia E.	May 5, 1847.			May 6, 1847.
4. Alice L.	March 2, 1848.	I. N. Tucker.	Sept. 22, 1872.	
5. Adelaide L.	Nov. 5, 1849.	James Dunn.	May 29, 1870.	
6. Adelbert E.	July 6, 1851.			
7. Addison A.	August 4, 1853.			
8. Aldaman D	Feb. 3, 1855.			
9. Allene A.	July 4, 1856.	James Kimmel.	May 14, 1884.	
10. Arloa A.	April 7, 1862.	Wm. R. Maloy.	July 4, 1882.	
11. Augustin H	Jan. 9, 1864.			Nov., 1864.

Horace Pardee is the eldest son of a respectable and wealthy farmer who resided in Harmony, Chautauqua county, N. Y. A few years after his marriage he removed to Kansas, before the breaking out of the Southern rebellion. Here the incipient conflict between slavery and freedom was inaugurated, and here some of the most cruel and barbarous acts of the war were perpetrated. His home was attacked by guerrilla bandits at different times, when a small quantity of household goods and a large quantity of children were pitched into two lumber wagons, he driving one team and his wife the other, and made his escape with his precious freight over the plains to lodge in some secluded cornfield, with no shelter but their wagons. Mr. Pardee, with his neighboring pioneers, organized themselves into a committee of safety, which was afterward recognized by the Government. These bold, fearless men, enraged by murder and plunder, went down upon the Missouri banditti like a pack of bloodhounds. They often sent them flying into their own state, where they captured and drove away large herds of cattle and horses.

Lieutenant Pardee carries the mark of Rebel lead in one of his hands, a wound received in one of those almost hand-to-hand conflicts with a guerrilla band. He is a rough-hewn man, but one of courage and great force of character.

Rachel, his wife, proved herself no less courageous and meritorious in her pioneer life. The little ones were always protected and cared for. Her humane principles and elevated sentiments were born and bred into her children so effectually that they are a family of worthy, useful citizens.

Amelia D. Pardee; born November 5, 1843.

(Present address, Eureka, Greenwood county, Kansas.)

George Ellis; born February 1, 1832.

They were married March 31, 1862.

George Ellis died May 1, 1864.

Charles E. McQueen, second husband; born September 2, 1840.

They were married November 20, 1866.

THEIR CHILDREN—NINTH GENERATION.

1. Arthur R. Ellis; born at Paola, Kansas, August 4, 1864.

2. Guy H. McQueen; born at Wolcottville, Indiana, January 22, 1868.

3. Bissie A. McQueen; born at Louisburg, Kansas, February 6, 1877.

George Ellis was a mechanic by occupation, and was noted for his manly deportment and generosity as a citizen. He was a First Lieutenant in the United States Army in the War of the Rebellion. He was also noted for his honor and bravery as an officer and soldier. He died from wounds received in battle. Ellis county and Ellis City were named in honor of this noble Lieutenant.

Charles E. McQueen is a farmer, a hard working, energetic, honest man, holding the confidence and esteem of his neighbors and the strongest affection and love of his wife and children.

Mrs. Amelia McQueen was fortunate in her birth, from being favored with more than ordinary development of intellectual faculties, well braced up by a perfect physical structure. She has been fortunate in the selection of two worthy men as husbands, and her prospects are now fair for a prosperous and useful life. Possessing a clear understanding of the world and its duties, she is prompt and active in every line of life before her. She is led to pity, rather than despise, the less favored children of humanity.

Alice L. Pardee; born March 2, 1848.
Isaac N. Tucker; born April 29, 1851.
They were married September 22, 1872.
(Address, Lodi, Barber county, Kansas.)

THEIR CHILDREN—NINTH GENERATION.

1. Ethelyn V.; born August 26, 1873, at Paola, Kansas.
2. Josiah D.; born January 10, 1876, at Kellogg, Iowa.

3. Eugene N.; born August 16, 1880, at Lodi, Kansas.
4. Ella E.; born September 12, 1882.

Adelaide L. Pardee; born November 5, 1849.
James Dunn; born ——.
They were married May 29, 1870.
(Address, Ottawa, Franklin county, Kansas.

NINTH GENERATION.

They have four children, of whom we have no record.

Allene A. Pardee; born July 14, 1856.
James Kimmel; born September 2, 1838.
They were married May 14, 1884.
(Address, Lodi, Barber county, Kansas.)

Arloa A. Pardee; born April 7, 1862.
William B. Maloy; born October 13, 1858.
They were married July 4, 1882.
(Address, Sheron, Barber county, Kansas.)

THEIR CHILD—NINTH GENERATION.

1. John A.; born September 22, 1883, in Medicine Lodge, Kansas.

William Walker, second son of Thomas D. Walker, was born in the town of Greene, Chenango county, N. Y., July 28, 1821.
(Address, Bearlake, Warren county, Pa.)

In his boyhood he displayed a talent for business above the ordinary gifts to mankind. At the period of his majority he bought a sawmill and a tract of pine timber, which by his energy and good management he paid for in a short time. While engaged in lumbering he entered into a co-partnership with his brother in-law, D W. Elderkin, in the mercantile business in 1850, which business was not a success. From the stringent condition of the times, many of their customers failed to pay up their debts and the firm lost several thousand dollars, which affected the company seriously in their finances. But with unshaken courage Mr Walker pursued his lumber business for several years with success. In the meantime he engaged as the leader of a company to raise the sunken hull of an emigrant boat that went down in Lake Erie, containing a safe with $100,000 in gold and silver. They built a wrecker in Buffalo and spent a year in their enterprise. They found the hull and hitched to her, and drew her half a mile toward shore, when the fastening broke and she was again left to the mercy of the wind and waves. When they found her again, she was too deeply imbedded in sand to be recovered, so there was another loss of several thousand dollars.

Mr. Walker, soon after this effort, bought a farm of 400 acres in the neighborhood of his present residence, where he bred and dealt extensively in fine stock. In this business he was very successful. He is now retired with sufficient means for old age. He is 5 feet 10 inches in height and weighs 165 pounds: is a fine looking man, with easy manners, affable address, and is a fluent conversationalist, mirthful in the selection of topics, calm and certain in government, generous to the poor and hospitable to his guests. He was a kind son to his aged mother, who leaned on his strong arm until the last moment of her life. His moral deportment is an example of chastity and fidelity worthy of imitation.

Mary M. (DeLong) Walker is one of those women who are a public blessing to the race. Her stability of mind and superior judgment do much to guide the weak and wavering in the community where she resides. Among her intimate acquaintances and friends she is a model of womanly graces. She speaks of the faults of the erring reluctantly, always noting some palliating circumstance in their case. She is well read in the substantial literature of the age. As a wife she has stood side by side with her husband as a counselor and helper, always doing her part well, and never frowning upon him in times of adversity. They are a happy family, having raised two sons and a young lady, Miss Velma Grace Doud.

They all belong to the Universal Church.

William Walker; born July 28, 1821.
Mary M. DeLong; born November 22, 1821.
They were married June 6, 1844.

THEIR CHILDREN—EIGHTH GENERATION.

NAMES.	BORN.	MARRIED TO.	DATE OF MAR.	DIED
1. Cecil E.	June 19, 1848.	Ello Curtis.	Nov. 5, 1870.	
2. Leon E.	Nov. 3, 1850.	Elma J. Spencer.	May, 1874.	

Cecil E. Walker was born June 19, 1848.
Ello Curtis was born November 3, 1850.
They were married November 5, 1870.
(Address, Bearlake, Warren county, Pa.)

THEIR SON—NINTH GENERATION.

1. Roy Curtis Walker; born in Freehold, Pa., April 8, 1874.

Cecil E. Walker is a farmer, occupying his father's old homestead. He resembles his father so nearly in his characteristics that a full description of him would be only a repetition of what has already been said.

Mrs. Ello Walker may well be an amiable, intellectual, kind woman, descending, as she did, from a union of the Curtis and Dewey families. Their son is a bright, intelligent boy.

Thus we see in the human family that affinity seeks its equal, and heredity, both physical and mental, passes down through the generations from age to age.

Leon Elmer Walker; born December 9, 1851.
Elma J. Spencer; born April 26, 1855.
They were married May, 1874.
(Address, Bearlake, Warren county, Pa.

THEIR SON—NINTH GENERATION.

1. Carl D. Walker; born in Freehold, Pa., August 23, 1876.

Leon E. Walker is also a farmer, living on a portion of his father's old estate. If possible, he possesses more energy and fervency of organization than was common to his ancestors. His stock is fine, his farming neat and always on time, and his residence a mansion that would be an honor to a large town. He is unlike his father, being inclined to taciturnity.

Mrs. Elma J. (Spencer) Walker came from a worthy parentage and brought to her husband's estate several thousand dollars. They are a well matched couple, both possessing the accumulative qualities of mind. Leon is a graduate of a commercial college, and in addition has a good common English education. Carl D. is another bright boy.

Through respect to Mrs. Mary M. (DeLong) Walker and her descendants, the writer has introduced into this work the following short sketch of the DeLong family:

Francis DeLong was a patriot and an officer in the Revolutionary war. He married Elizabeth Wells, both of Connecticut. They raised a large family, the third son's name being Jacob.

Jacob DeLong married Anna Underwood.

THEIR CHILDREN—SEVENTH GENERATION.

1. Emma L.; married Ira Pearse and had a family.
2. Elizabeth W.
3. Anna M.
4. Elias Ruel; married and had a family.
5. Anna E.
6. Mary M.; married Wm. Walker and raised a family.
7. Electa Jane.
8. Jacob Albert.

Of the descendants of the DeLong family, one of them is noted as an Arctic explorer, and one as a minister of the Gospel.

Augustin Hays Walker; born November 1, 1826.
Married C. R. Barker February 22, 1849.
Married Louisa H. Freeman January 14, 1854.
C. R. Walker died May 8, 1852.
Augustin H. Walker died April 23, 1880.

CHILDREN OF A. H. AND LOUISA WALKER—EIGHTH GENERATION.

1. Elvene M.
2. Alene C.
3. Ella L.

THE KING FAMILY.

The first that we hear of the King family of Cherry Creek, Chautauqua county, N. Y., is in Rhode Island in 1769. Ward and Wanton King were twin brothers. Ward removed to Massachusetts, where he married Sally Walker, who was born in New Hampshire. They lived in Massachusetts until they had a family of eight children, when Ward and Wanton (Romulus and Remus like), started for the far west to locate the site of their future homes. They bid adieu to their friends on the 3d of February, 1817, and with three ox teams and sleds made their journey across the state of New York to Chautauqua county in twenty days, where they landed in the town of Ellington on the 23d of the same month. Their site was chosen, not by the flight of birds, but from the beautiful flats that skirt the valley of the Conewango creek on its western border, near Cherry creek, one of its tributaries. This valley, about four miles wide and twenty miles long, is the bed of an ancient lake, which became drained off from washing away of the outlet at Waterborough. Here the hills are over one hundred feet high with rapid descent to water's edge. Below this outlet the stream for half a mile is called the Conewango Rapids. From Cherry Creek to the outlet of this defunct lake is about ten miles, yet the winding, vermicular course of the Conewango measured a distance of about thirty miles. In the bed of this stream, fifteen feet below the surface, are seen the bodies of trees sticking out from the banks in a state of complete preservation. The ages only can tell when those water-soaked trees found their final resting place in the bottom of that beautiful sheet of water, on whose bosom that

Indian's bark floated of whom we have no legend. In this wild, romantic and beautiful valley Ward and Wanton King took up their farms and erected their humble cabins within about one hundred rods of each other. Here they raised their families. Here they lived to see the growth and progress of the country around them, and here they enjoyed more of life than a Cæsar or an Alexander. In their old age, it is said, they usually met once a day for a sit-down visit, when each would relate some of the same old anecdotes, to as complete entertainment of both as though they were entirely new. Soon after the settlement of the Kings, Mr. Kent came in with a large family and joined them as a neighbor. From this time the settlement increased rapidly, and Cherry Creek became a hamlet with a variety store, postoffice, hotel, school house, blacksmith shop, etc. Here the people, full of patriotism and love of country, assembled with fife and drum on the Fourth of July to celebrate their victory over old England, and the glories of the land of the free and the home of the brave. This state of things may look insignificant compared to the pomp and display of present demonstrations, but these pioneer settlements were the corner stones of all the greatness and grandeur of our now magnificent country. Those were noble blooded men. They were brave, persistent, strong minded, honest people, who voted for General Jackson, honest government and equal rights. The Kings, Kents, Greenes, Bentleys and others intermarried and raised families to such an extent in and about Cherry Creek that a visitor cannot make a tour of the relationship in a period of six weeks. As a family and connection they are well provided with the necessities, conveniences and comforts of life. In fact, most of them enjoy all the luxuries of life that afford healthful and abiding pleasure. Their nicely painted farmhouses are furnished with carpets, instruments of music and upholstered furniture. Their neat and spacious barns are alive with fine stock and supplied with carriages, harnesses and robes. They live at home, ride in their own carriages of ease and splendor, and sleep without dreams of financial crashes.

Ward King was born in West Greenwich, R. I., February, 1769.

Sally Walker was born in New Hampshire May, 1776.

They were married 1795.

Ward King died August, 1848.

Sally King died January, 1858.

THEIR CHILDREN—SEVENTH GENERATION.

NAMES.	BORN.	MARRIED TO.	DATE OF MAR.	DIED.
1. Susan.	April, 1796.	Benj. Bentley.	Jan., 1816	June, 1873.
2. Wanton.	Oct., 1798.	Martha Popple.	Jan., 1823.	July, 1869.
3. Ward, Jr.	May 12, 1801.	Dolly Kent.	Nov., 1828.	Dec. 15, 1886.
4. Lydia.	June, 1804.	Wm. Kelbourne.	Oct. 7, 1824.	1886
5. James.	July, 1806.	Car'line Waterberry	Oct., 1834.	May, 1873.
6. Hiram.	Dec., 1809	Catherine Graves.	Nov., 1837.	
7. Norman.	July, 1813.	Pamelia Watson.	Nov., 1840.	May, 1879.
8. Benjamin,	July, 1816.	Laura Pendleton.	Sept., 1843.	
9. Sally.	June, 1820.	Wm. Pendleton.	Oct., 1849.	

Of this family all had children except Norman and Sally. The connection is too extensive for the design of this work, and therefore we will only introduce the families of Ward, Jr., and Benjamin.

Ward King, Jr., was born May 12, 1801.

Dolly Kent was born October 7, 1809.

They were married November, 1828.

Dolly King died November, 1856.

Ward King, Jr., died December 15, 1886.

THEIR CHILDREN—EIGHTH GENERATION.

NAMES.	BORN.	MARRIED TO.	DATE OF MAR.	DIED.
1. Jane A.	March 17, 1829.	Lester J. Martin.	April 4, 1850.	
2. Lois.	August 13, 1830.	Dyer W. Elderkin	Aug. 22, 1854.	
3. Eliza.	Nov. 9, 1832.	Hopkins Carr.	Nov. 21, 1858.	
4. Lyman.	March 1, 1833.	Harriet R. Martin.	Oct. 19, 1856.	
5. George.				In infancy.
6. John.	March 29, 1838.	1st, Nora Walker.	Oct. 25, 1859.	
		2d, C. Schermerhorn	June 9, 1872.	
7. Lucy.	Feb. 10, 1839.	1st, Delos Carl	May 13, 1860.	
		2d, Delbert Bentley.	Dec. 11, 1880.	
8. Laura A.	Nov. 22, 1840.	J. B. Shattuck.	Sept. 7, 1862.	
9. William.	April 16, 1844.	Laura A. Bently.	May 17, 1873.	
10. Willard.	April 16, 1844.	Died a	Union soldier.	Nov., 1863.

Ward King, Jr., was a farmer and mechanic. He conducted his farm in a very neat style during the summer season, and spent the winter in his shop making chairs and other useful articles. He raised a large and respectable family, who are all getting on finely in the comforts and conveniences of life. He died December 18th, 1886, at the age of eighty-five years, at his home at Cherry Creek, Chautauqua county, New York.

Mrs. Dolly King came from a good family of stirring, enterprising people. Two of her brothers were engaged extensively in manufacturing and shipping lumber, and one of her cousins has been a banker in Jamestown, New York, for nearly fifty years. She was a kind mother and highly respected lady. She died from a cancer in the breast.

Jane A. King; born at Cherry Creek, N. Y., March 17, 1829.

Lester J. Martin; born October 28, 1828.

They were married April 4, 1850.

(Address, Lincolnville, Crawford county, Pa.)

THEIR CHILDREN—NINTH GENERATION.

NAMES.	BORN.	MARRIED TO.	DATE OF MAR.	DIED.
1. Charles E.	March 13, 1860.	Adda Ray Oakes.	April 7, 1885.	
2. Willis A.	October 5, 1861.	Anna A. Farrington	Jan. 3, 1883	
3. Frank L.	May 16, 1864.			April 26, 1866.
4. Carrie A.	May 26, 1867.	John Foxburg.	Dec. 31, 1885.	

Lester J. Martin is a farmer and merchant, a keen, shrewd business man. He is reliable and prompt in all his engagements, and has accumulated a nice estate. He engages in no neighborhood bickerings, is kind in his family and a trustworthy friend.

Charles E. Martin; born at Lincolnville, March 13, 1860.

Adda R. Oakes; born in Wayne township, October 14, 1861.

They were married April 7, 1885.

(Address, Lincolnville, Crawford county, Pa.)

THEIR CHILD—TENTH GENERATION.

1. Marie; born March 2, 1886.

Charles E. Martin is 5 feet 11 inches in height, and weighs 170 pounds. Is a stirring business man, conducting the business of a general dry goods, grocery and variety store at Lincolnville. He has charge of the postoffice also.

Mrs. Addie Martin's height is 5 feet 6 inches; weight, 148 pounds. She was born in Wayne township, Crawford county, Pa., attended high school in Meadville, Pa., also State Normal School at Edinboro, and graduated in music at Chamberlain Institute, Randolph, New York, in June, 1882. Her father's name, David H. Oakes; mother's name, Eliza (Baldwin) Oakes. He died a Union soldier, January 30, 1865. Her mother married O. B. Cravens, with whom Addie lived until her marriage. She is cool deliberate and substantial in her organization, refined in manners, and practical in the duties of life.

Willis A. Martin; born at Lincolnville, October 5, 1861.
Anna A. Farrington.
They were married January 3, 1883.
(Address, Riceville, Crawford county, Pa.)
They have no children.

Willis A. Martin is over six feet in height and weighs 180 pounds. He is a farmer, with nice house, barn and fixtures. He is pleasant, companionable and honest, and a good citizen.

His wife is tall, slender and amiable, a lady in every sense of the word. They have the faculty of making their guests feel at home and the darkest day brilliant with the light of life and cheerful song. They both play on the piano.

Carrie A. Martin; born May 26, 1867.
John Foxburg.
They were married December 31, 1885.
(Address, Lincolnville, Crawford county, Pa.)

John and Carrie are a well bred couple, who have their footprints yet to make in the sands of the future. We believe they will succeed well.

Lois King; born in Cherry Creek, August 31, 1830.
Dyer W. Elderkin; born in Livingston county, N. Y., April 9, 1817.
(Address, Spartansburg, Crawford county, Pa.)
Their record can be found in Chapter VIII. of this work.

Hopkins Carr; born September 12, 1828.
Matilda Kilborne, first wife; born October 10, 1829.

Eliza King, second wife; born November 9, 1832.

First marriage, December 27, 1848.

Second marriage, to Eliza King, November 21, 1858.

Mrs. Matilda Carr died May 22, 1858.

(Address, Cherry Creek, Chautauqua county, N. Y.)

CHILDREN BY FIRST WIFE—NINTH GENERATION.

1. Sarah; born September 26, 1849; married A. B. Johnson, August 4, 1873.

2. Clyrinda; born March 11, 1851; married Z. E. Douglas, March 8, 1870.

3 and 4 died in infancy.

CHILD BY SECOND WIFE.

5. Nason; born February 20, 1861; died October 6, 1865.

Hopkins Carr is a retired farmer, with means enough to live as he pleases. His integrity of character has secured the confidence and esteem of his townsmen, and his good judgment renders him useful to the weak and wavering.

Mrs. Eliza Carr is a very large and fine looking woman. She weighs 220 pounds, and is noted for the neatness and style of her household affairs.

Sarah Carr; born September 26, 1849.

A. B. Johnson.

They were married August 4, 1873.

(Address, Cottage, Cattaraugus county, N. Y.)

THEIR CHILDREN—TENTH GENERATION.

1. Cora; born April 25, 1874.

2. Lora; born August 20, 1878.

They are nice people.

Clyrinda Carr; born March 11, 1851.
Z. E. Douglas.
They were married March 8, 1870.
(Address, Fredonia, Chautauqua county, N. Y.)

THEIR CHILDREN—TENTH GENERATION.

1. Lula; born November 12, 1874.
2. Orton; born June 9, 1876.

This is another fine family.

Lyman King: born at Cherry Creek, March 1, 1833.
Harriet R. Martin; born Feb. 4, 1833.
They were married October 19, 1856.
(Address, Riceville, Crawford county, Pa.)

THEIR CHILDREN—NINTH GENERATION.

NAMES.	BORN.	MARRIED TO.	DATE OF MAR.	DIED.
1. Clara D.	October 21, 1857.			Nov. 1, 1860.
2. Frank R.	Sept. 7, 1860.			Mar. 31, 1861.
3. Edith A.	Nov. 12, 1863.	Ruba F. Edwards.	Dec. 13, 1883	

Lyman King is six feet tall and weighs 180 pounds He is a successful farmer, having built up a fine residence and spacious outbuildings. He is a deep, profound thinker, and reasons on science, the arts and politics. Mrs. Harriet King is an educated woman, with a clear mind on business matters. Her aid and counsel have been of value to her husband, as they have traveled up the rugged path of life to a happy old age. She is well read in the literature of the day.

Edith A. King; born at Riceville, November 12, 1863.
Ruba F. Edwards; born in Indiana, February 2, 1859.
They were married December 13, 1883.
(Address, Riceville, Crawford county, Pa.)

R F. Edwards lived at Panama, Chautauqua county, N. Y., until he was eleven years old. Since that time he has resided at Riceville. He had the advantages of a first-class English education. His employment was teaching before he was married. He is now engaged in farming. He is very energetic in business and very economical.

Mrs. Edith Edwards also has a good common education. She is a good organist and well versed in the management of household affairs. They are a well matched couple and will pull together on the same end of the rope. They reside with her parents, and conduct the affairs of the farm and home under the supervision of Mr. and Mrs. King, who are not yet too old to make themselves useful.

John King; born in Cherry Creek, March 29, 1838.

Nora Walker, first wife; born February 16, 1836.

Mrs. Clarissa Schermerhorn, second wife; born April 20, 1832.

Married to first wife October 25, 1859.

Married to second wife June 9, 1872.

Mrs. Nora King died July 5, 1871.

(Address, Cherry Creek, Chautauqua county, N. Y.)

CHILDREN BY FIRST MARRIAGE—NINTH GENERATION.

1. Albert; born May 22, 1861.
2. Dolly; born January 28, 1865.

John King is a medium sized man of good habits and a kind, generous, companionable disposition. He is the clown of the King race, running over full of witty jokes, jests and puns. He is the life and entertainment of every party and circle that is favored with his presence. He is a farmer and mechanic. His development in mechanism is so great that he can construct and build all classes of machinery without having learned a trade.

Mrs. King possesses a superior financial ability. By putting their heads together they get along nicely.

Lucy King; born in Cherry Creek, February 10, 1839.
Delos Carl, first husband; born December 10, 1832.
Delbert Bentley, second husband; born March 10, 1851.
Married to Delos Carl May 13, 1860.
Married to Delbert Bentley December 11, 1880.
Delos Carl died April 16, 1874.
(Address, Cherry Creek, Chautauqua county, N. Y.)

CHILDREN BY FIRST HUSBAND—NINTH GENERATION.

1. Ulric Carl; born December 1, 1863.
2. Minnie Carl; born May 11, 1865.

Delos Carl was a good man for one of his organization, which was a highly nervous temperament. He was quick to observe and draw conclusions, easily excited, and endowed with a gift of language to express all he felt. Was industrious and a good provider.

Mr. Bentley is mild, kind and agreeable at home or abroad. His politeness and gentility in his own house make sunshine for his wife and their guests.

Mrs. Lucy Bentley is 5 feet 7 inches in height; weight, 210 pounds. She is a very fine looking and fashionable lady. She is the principal correspondent of the family, reporting births, marriages, condition of health and general progress among the connection. Distant visitors never think a visit complete until they have called on Lucy. She possesses a will power superior to dictation, and is consequently self-reliant in all her purposes and acts.

Minnie Carl; born at Cherry Creek, May 11, 1865.
Hoyt F. Smith.
They were married September 28, 1881.
(Address, Cherry Creek, Chautauqua county, N. Y.)

Mr. Smith is a carpenter and house joiner.
Mrs. Smith is educated in English branches and music.

Laura Aurilla King; born November 22, 1840.
Jerome B. Shattuck; born May 27, 1841.
They were married September 7, 1862.
(Address, Cherry Creek, Chautauqua county, N. Y.)

THEIR CHILDREN—NINTH GENERATION.

NAMES.	BORN.	MARRIED TO.	DATE OF MAR.	DIED
1. Plinna.	June 21, 1863.			
2. Dolly.	June 13, 1867.			Aug. 12, 1870.
3. Nine M.	July 17, 1871.			
4. Flos.	Dec. 4, 1876.			
5. John F.	July 10, 1879.			

Jerome B. Shattuck is a very energetic business farmer. He deals extensively in fine imported stock, and winters from fifty to eighty head of cattle, besides sheep and hogs. His organ of acquisitiveness is large, and his judgment on stock and finances equal to his desire.

Mrs. Shattuck is well adapted to her husband's business, being industrious and economical, always with her lamps trimmed and burning for early breakfasts and late suppers. They are strictly a business family, who find little time for visiting and social life.

William King; born at Cherry Creek, April 16, 1844.
Laura A. Bentley; born at Cherry Creek, April 1, 1846.
They were married May 17, 1873.
(Address, Cherry Creek, Chautauqua county, N. Y.)

THEIR CHILD—NINTH GENERATION.

1. Linnie A.; born May 10, 1879.

William King is a large, strong man, who spent ten

years in a saw mill and in the lumbering business before he was married, when he bought a farm and settled down to a more regular and easy life. He is industrious and economical, and enjoys a large share of happiness in his comfortable home. He is a man of strong mind and good judgment. In his selection of a wife he locked arms with one of the finest women of whom Cherry Creek can boast. She is open hearted, frank, candid, free from disguise, equivocation or dissimulation. Their little daughter is a remarkable child for brightness of intellect, beauty of person and womanly deportment.

Benjamin King, the eighth child of Ward King, Sr., was born in the town of Hancock, Berkshire county, Mass., July 23, 1816.

Laura Pendleton was born in the town of Ellengton, Chautauqua county, N. Y., April 7, 1823.

They were married September 28, 1843.

(Address, Cherry Creek, Chautauqua county, N. Y.)

THEIR CHILDREN—EIGHTH GENERATION.

NAMES.	BORN.	MARRIED TO.	DATE OF MAR.	DIED.
1. Vinal H.	Oct. 20, 1844.	Ella G. Sage.	July 1, 1865.	
2. Eli W.	July 12, 1855.	Mary M. Parsons.	Jan. 1, 1883.	

Benjamin King and his brother, Norman, continued to occupy the old homestead many years after the death of their father, which was ten years previous to the death of their mother, who lived with them. Benjamin finally bought out his brother and erected a fine residence on the same site where he had lived from his infancy. He is a short, small sized man, one of the precious packages whose value cannot be determined by its weight. He is not loquacious, but always acts sociable and genial. His promise to pay is as good as a bank draft. His opinions on public or private affairs are considered standard. His home has been the grand hailing point of all the connection; his latch string is ever out and barn doors open to welcome all who are attracted by the ties of affinity or consanguinity. "Uncle Benjamin" is honored and respected by all who know him. His companionable nature prompts him to visit his friends as well as to receive them, and he will take time to go in spite of business pressure.

"Aunt Laura's" height is 5 feet 8 inches; weight, 180 pounds. She was vigorous and healthy during her younger days, and could care for more company than two common women. It was hard to tell whether her hands or tongue could fly the faster. The more the merrier with Aunt Laura. By her wit she keeps surprise and merriment on the wing, thereby carrying the minds of her guests away from the dull cares of life into the realms of mirthful fancy. Her memory is so tenacious that she reproduces past events with almost as complete accuracy as if they were registered. At that old home where grandmother cooked venison and wild turkeys, and which grandfather guarded with firebrands and his rifle from the encroachments of wolves, panthers and wild cats, the writer has spent some of the happiest visiting days of his life. Long may uncle and aunt live to reap the rewards of a useful life.

Vinal King, born in Ellington, October 20, 1884.

Ella G. Sage, born in Hanover, July 28, 1846.

They were married July 1, 1865.

(Address, Cherry Creek, Chautauqua county, N. Y.)

THEIR CHILD—NINTH GENERATION.

Louisa L., born December 28, 1872.

Mr. King is a tall, large man, and a good citizen. Mrs. King is a sprightly little woman.

Eli W. King, born in Ellington, July 12, 1855.
Mary M. Parsons, born in Charlotte, July, 1854.
They were married January 1, 1883.
(Address, Cherry Creek, Chautauqua county, N. Y.)

THEIR CHILD—NINTH GENERATION.

Benjamin, born 1885.

Eli W. King is the largest man in Cherry Creek. He married a tall, fine looking, smart woman. They live with his parents at the old homestead.

Mr. and Mrs. Kent, parents of Mrs. Ward King, Jr., raised their family at Cherry Creek, Chautauqua county, N. Y. He was wounded in the knee in the war of 1812, the point always remaining stiff.

THEIR CHILDREN—SEVENTH GENERATION.

NAMES.	BORN.	MARRIED TO.	DATE OF MAR.	DIED.
1. George.		Phebe King.		
2. Nancy.		Eliphalet Wilcox.		
3. Dolly.	Oct. 7, 1809.	Ward King, Jr.	Nov., 1828.	Nov., 1856.
4. Elisha.		Lydia Wyard.		
5. Sam'l Brazil		Charlotte T. Greene		
6. Joseph.		2. Rachel Vador.		
7. Polly.		——— Hines.		
8. Lydia.		Hon. Chas. Greene.		
9. Ara W.				

The writer has the pleasure of a personal acquaintance with some of the members of this family, but at this time is not in possession of their records. Samuel Brazil and Joseph engaged extensively in lumbering. Joseph Kent, though poorly educated, was a clear thinker and reasoner, active in politics and a representative man in Cherry Creek. He gave employment for many years to a large gang of men. S. Brazil Kent conducted his business within a smaller circle, but accumulated the most money. A short time before his death he had invested largely in the pine timber lands of Michigan. While on his way from Cherry Creek to his mills in that State he was found dead in bed at a hotel.

Mrs. Charlotte Kent is a woman who has few equals. She is a large woman, with large head and large powers of research and comprehension. She is social, amiable and dignified. Her merits are especially appreciated by persons of education and refinement.

They have no children.

Hon. Charles Greene, a brother of Mrs S. B. Kent, is an attorney and counselor-at-law, admitted to the Supreme Courts. He was twice elected to the Legislature of the State of New York, and officiated as a recruiting officer for the United States Army in the War of the Rebellion. He is extensively read in the history and biography of our country, and well posted in natural science. He is an agreeable companion, inclined to mirthful anecdotes and entertaining reminiscences.

Mrs Lydia (Kent) Greene had all the good qualities of a first-class wife and mother. She died several years ago, leaving two sons, Daniel and Charles Hon. Charles Greene now lives with his sister, Charlotte Kent, at Cherry Creek, Chautauqua county, N. Y.

APPENDIX.

ORIGINAL THEORIES ON SCIENTIFIC SUBJECTS.

These articles or theories on some points of science are original so far as the writer has any knowledge. The same ideas may have been advanced at some previous time or in some other place, but if so they never reached me. I am aware that some portions of them are opposed to the generally accepted theories of to-day. But they are my ideas, based upon a careful course of scientific reasoning, and I humbly submit them to the criticism of the scientific world, to stand or fall as they may prove true or false by the light of progressive knowledge.

My original discovery of the Origin, Progress and Cure of Pulmonary Consumption, I believe to be one of the great blessings given to mankind. The nature of the disease has never been known to the medical faculty. On this discovery I have been greatly wronged by a friend, James M. Bunn, M. D , who borrowed my manuscript to test the truth of my theory, and went before the annual meeting of the Electric Medical Association of the State of Pennsylvania, and read my theory, combined with some ideas of his own, as his original article on pulmonary consumption. As such it was published in the "Keystone Medical Journal" of August, 1884. Afterwards it was read before the National Medical Association at Cincinnati. I have Dr. Bunn's letters to prove that he received the manuscript from me.

These theories have all been published at different times in newspapers, except the theory on Consumption, and some of them have been well received by men of ability.

Of their worth or merits each must judge for himself.

D. W. Elderkin,

Professor of Natural Sciences and Attorney-at-Law.

Spartansburg, Pa.

ERRORS OF ASTRONOMY.

In attempting to investigate the physical laws of nature, which lie concealed in the obscurity of distance, or are not brought within tangible perception through the media of our senses, the first great work to be done is to base the foundation of our reasoning upon a hypothesis which is true. The question to-day is, have astronomers laid such a foundation?

The first great untenable position in astronomy is the assumption of a beginning, a creation! This hypothesis leads to the conclusion that there was a period previous to said creation when there was no creation, no beginning, no organization.

This theory involves the question of material out of which to create; the method, medium or process by which this creation was carried on to completion; the magnitude of the work accomplished, the space occupied; locality selected, the condition before the beginning; and the motor power that developed this visible structure of the universe.

The second assumption is, that there existed in, and through the inconceivable ages of a goneby eternity, a self-existing, independent, uncreated being, who by the power of his word could, and did change darkness into light, and nothing into something; and that something into shining orbs, planets and satelites; and all into a gloomy universe, swarming with incomprehensible forms of life, from man to the molecule.

The legitimate inferences to be drawn from this hypothesis depend upon the analysis of the premises. If eternity had no beginning, no back end to it, can it be any older in one age, stage or period than in any other? If not, then the past ages of eternity are as old as a whole eternity, and this creation must have existed during all the eternity, or the work must have been begun after an eternity of idleness had passed. By what law did this eternal slumbering power wake up, and from a state of perpetual idleness create a universe from nothing? How much nothing does it take to make one something, and how much less of nothing remained after a universe had been created out of it?

If darkness was changed into light at any special period then this creative power previous to that time must have had his wings of endless light folded up like the unhatched eagle in his shell, with his omnipotent attributes rolled together like a scroll, while he, perched upon a twig of nothing in the midst of infinite space, slept the eternal night away.

The third vague assumption is, "that there once existed in space a great, chaotic, nebulous mass, endowed with a kind of whirlpool motion, which, gradually condensing through the mutual attraction of its particles, formed the countless suns distributed through space; that the planets were formed by the condensation of rings of matter successfully thrown off by the central mass, and the satellites by the condensation of matter thrown off in like manner by their primaries."

This nebulous theory as an original beginning implies a creation and a period before creation, the incipient state of matter, a lack of duration in the bygone eternity to mature or ripen matter fit for planet making.

The whole great folly of a beginning, conception, birth, growth, maturity, age and decay of matter or of a universe or universes must be discarded, swept away, wiped out before we can proceed with any degree of consistency, to lay our foundation for astronomical investigation upon a basis of truth that will stand the test of the present condition of matter.

Take this hypothesis: Unbounded, unlimited, infinite

space was not made, but always was, and is, without regard to time and eternity.

Space always was, and is, and will be occupied by great central masses of matter held in clusters or universes by the laws of attraction and repulsion.

Matter cannot be created, nor annihilated ; but under certain conditions subjects itself to change of form and location.

A great unlimited intelligence pervades, permeates and actuates all matter, which is as incomprehensible to man as the power that dictates his own mind.

Electricity is nature's agent, the dispenser of light and heat ; the power is motion and attraction.

Electricity is a material substance varying in its constituent parts from two materials adapted to a certain work, or office, to a union of every element that enters into the molecular structure of the universe. It may be weak or strong, positive or negative, attractive or repulsive, active or sluggish, according to condition, or purpose to be accomplished. A portion of it is solidified into every species of organized masses which enter into the organization of a solar system. Portions of it may be, and they are attenuated through the immensity of space.

With the preceding declaration it is believed that every condition of matter in the illimitable universes can be accounted for. About 20,000,000 of stars are visible to the astronomers of this planet. They are all suns like our own, with slight variations shining from their own electric light, and believed to be the centers of systems of primary and secondary planets and comets. The size of them will probably average more than a million times larger than the earth we live on. They are all moving in a great circular orbit around a common center in space. Each sun is heated to an incandescent state. When, why and how they are heated are unsettled questions. Our answer to the when is, they were always hot; to the why and how, that the gravitation of their own mass toward a common center produces a pressure and friction of particles sufficient to evolve latent heat enough to liquify the whole body, and convert the metals on their surfaces into vapor, which is carried away by electric repulsion, through the broad interstices between their lines of perpetual march. Why are not these suns moving in parallel lines with each other, by the law of gravitation, drawn together and consolidated into one great central mass?

Being hot they are each positively electrified and repel each other.

The diffusion of matter from the suns by electric repulsion accounts for the nebulous formations that appear in the heavens. These thin clouds lose their angry repulsive nature by cooling down while floating in space at so great a distance from home; attraction regains the ascendency and the work of reconstruction begins; first into dense clouds; second, collections of those clouds; third, consolidation of the first collections; fourth, union of those organized masses. After thousands of years of this kind of gathering up and enlargement by accretion, the mass is attracted toward the nearest sun, and would fall directly into it if the sun stood still; but as the machinery is all in motion, it whirls around the sun, becoming surcharged with electricity, gives the great electric parent a repulsive kick, and dashes off in its eccentric orbit to gather again the floating waste to its own bosom. This stranger is a comet, and this is its first trip around a sun, but not the last. It will continue to collect and consolidate matter, and make its periodical revolutions around the sun till it becomes a young brother planet on the outer circle of a solar system. Age solidifies organized matter. As the density of a planet increases by age, the distance from the sun decreases; hence, the oldest planet is nearest the sun, and the youngest farthest off. By the same process satellites and aerolites are formed. If any are fearful that our suns will shine themselves all away, they will find relief in the fact that all the expanded matter will ultimately find its home at the great original fountains.

As every planet is undergoing a process of consolidation, each particle pressing harder and closer to the common center of gravity, so every system of planets is advancing slowly, but no less surely, toward its center of attraction. When the nearest planet will have wound up its orbit, and excoriated the crusty surface of the sun with its mass of condensed electricity, those old gorges of dross that have obscured its brightness for ages will be dissolved, and a new glow of grandeur light up a flame of electric energy to other coming worlds, which, in turn, will receive their light and heat, motion and attraction from this great central perpetuity.

This theory clears up the nebulous formation, the creation of the planetary systems, moons and aerolites, the location of the planets in orbits at distances from the sun corresponding to their age and relative gravity, and the geological changes that take place in the stratification of a world by a constant accretion, and a continued change of vegetable and animal life, as the planet winds up from the remote, cold regions of space, nearer the great central mass of electric flames, increasing its volume of light and heat, which add greater activity, power, symmetry and beauty to all forms of life from the tertiary formations to the present condition of our world. This earth is increasing in size every day by falling aerolites and the condensation of gasses. The idea that our world was made up into a red-hot ball about six thousand years ago, and thrown out into its present orbit, where it has been cooling off till it has formed a crust from twenty-five to fifty miles thick, deserves nothing better than derision and contempt. If the central part is heated to a state of liquifaction, its cause is attractive pressure.

The law of attraction is a universal law when matter is in a condition to be attracted, and the law of repulsion is also universal when matter is in a condition to be repelled. In the growth of vegetation, the laws of attraction, affinity and assimilation act upon the particles of matter, bringing them together and uniting them in one common mass. These masses, subjected to other conditions, dissolve and repel their own once homogeneous particles with greater rapidity and energy than is manifested in the laws of organization. Here is displayed the law of evolution or repulsion.

On the law of involution or attraction, which makes particles of matter homogeneous, and the law of evolution or repulsion, which makes the same particles heterogeneous, rest the whole theory of planetary organization.

The great luminous orbs of the universes are undergoing a rapid electro-chemical decomposition upon their surfaces, producing a condition when repulsion snatches the wand of power that attraction held over the particles of matter, and hurls them from their moorings with a dash of electric energy that diffuses them throughout space.

Electricity, which displays the greatest activity when organized under repulsive influences, lies down as quiet as a lamb under the power of attractive combinations. To-day we see it tearing down from the clouds, splitting and rending every subject of its power before it, followed by peals of thunder that cause the earth to tremble; to-morrow we find it slumbering silently in the embrace of a sheet of zinc, copper and a quart of acid. Now we behold it gently agitating our atmosphere, throwing its genial warmth and light upon all animal and vegetable life; then its power is seen whirling and dashing that same atmosphere with such fury as to devastate towns and rob the forest of its foliage. What is this mysterious, slumbering, belching power, called electricity? It is the essence of all elementary matter, the finest unfolding of material substance. It holds in its embrace all the formative elements of worlds. It is the glow of the sunlight, the color in the rainbow and the beauty in flowers. It is the power that moves the muscular structure of animal organizations, and dissolves and unites compounds in chemistry. It carries from the luminous orbs of our universe to this earth samples of the metals of which they are composed, as exhibited through the medium of the spectroscope. The sun is hot and positively electrified. The earth is comparatively cold and negatively electrified. Hence, by the law of electrical attraction, the latter is tied to the former. The earth is warm compared to the moon, and is positive to that body, which ties the moon to the earth.

D. W. ELDERKIN.

Spartansburg, Pa., March 20th, 1883.

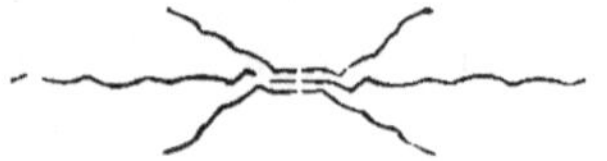

ELECTRICITY.

Atoms of matter which have extension in three directions, length, breadth and thickness, seem to be the smallest division of material nature that philosophers have had any conception of. In converting sandstone into glass the pebbles are fused by heat and reduced to a liquid mass. So, also, of other substances that may be reduced from a solid to a liquid fluid or gaseous form. In these conditions the atomic and molecular structures remain undissolved. From this fact it has been claimed that matter cannot be subjected to a state of divisibility finer than atoms. These atoms are supposed to be solids, and to possess an inherent vibratory motion or pulsation. It has been taught and believed that without this atomic organization matter cannot exist. I claim that matter in the form of that subtle agent called electricity contains no particles, molecules or atoms, all having been dissolved to a perfect state of fluidity. It is impressible to the slightest force, and flows without globules, slides without surfaces, and moves in and through all organized matter with greater or less facility. It holds about the same comparative relation to other matter, so far as fluidity is concerned, that water holds to wheat. When it is organized at the surface of one of our incandescent suns, electricity is composed of all the elementary substances on that surface whose atoms are broken down to the fluid state. Electricity flows off from the sun in the form of a great balloon, expanding its area and becoming more attenuated as it advances from a centre toward an unlimited circumference. As the outer surface expands, rarefaction follows in an increased ratio, weakening the force and losing motion till it finally comes to a state of rest, where it mingles with other diffused electric matter and forms the nebula referred to in a former article. It has no conductor to transmit it through space. It needs none, being thrown from the sun by a repulsive force that would make nitro-glycerine blush and turn pale with weakness. This flow from the sun's surface is constant and equal and uniform, except from patches of debris composed of recrement, scoria or dross, floating upon the surface of this liquid, seething, eradiating centralization of matter. Solar electricity produces all the vitalizing effects in and about our earth. It is light in the atmosphere, motion in the wind, lightning in the clouds and warmth upon the surface of the ground. The earth is the great reservoir and organizer of that portion of solar electricity which reaches its surface, and when portions of it are drawn from the earth by friction machines it resembles the original in quality and power more fully than any other production. That kind that is produced by chemical action is more voluminous, that is, rarified, and consequently weaker than the mother tinctures.

The human body is a little world which generates by heat, friction and chemical actions its own electric motor power. If our physicians generally understood that what they call nervous debility is simply electric exhaustion, and knew nature's methods of recuperation, how easily they might restore vigor to their waning patients. Assuming that all electricities are alike, and that they have some invisible medical property in them, thousands of experiments have been tried by forcing metalic and machine lightning into and through the bodies of sick and lame people, who were made seven times more the children of grief than they were before.

Animal electricity is rare, weak and slow in its movements. The brain is the battery. Sleep is the normal condition for recuperation. Respiration, digestion and circulation are the principal methods by which the battery is replenished. The nerves conduct the current or charge to the muscle where the force or motory power is applied.

A muscle is a bundle of fibres inclosed in a thin cellular membrane and attached at the head to a superior bone. It is large in the middle, tapering down toward the tail, where it changes its red color to white, forming a tendon which is inserted into an inferior bone below the joint. The fibres or threads of a muscle are made up of a series of rings extending from one end to the other When we desire to contract a muscle and thereby move a limb or a member of our body, the organ of firmness in the cerebrum, located near the crown of the head, applies a current of electricity to the nerve which is connected to the muscle inserted into the part to be moved. The electricity flowing upon the rings of the fibres expands their circumference, thereby rendering them thinner longitudinally, and consequently shorter, causing the point of insertion to move toward the point of attachment. Thus we raise our arm, shut our hand and move our limbs. Great electric shocks in our systems are from the cerebral battery.

When the blood flows to the brain in uniform healthy quantities, the electric governor has complete control of his battery, but when, from cardiac or arterial debility, or other cause, the brain is emptied of blood, the person faints or falls down with an epileptic fit. A horizontal position will restore the equilibrium in case of syncope, and relieve the symptom. But in epilepsy greater effort is required. The whole charge of the cerebral battery is thrown upon the motor nerves, simultaneously causing every muscle of voluntary motion to contract at the same time. The stronger muscles, to a great extent, predominate over the weaker. The head and shoulders are drawn back, the arms and hands forward and inward, the legs backward, with a winding, twisting, vermicular movement, producing the contortions and clonic spasms manifested in the falling sickness. The tension produced upon the muscular system by such a shock of electric energy appears to be nature's own method of forcing the blood from the extremities back to the brain again. Great physical force or power is produced by expending a corresponding quantity of electricity upon the muscles. The base brain contains the intelligence and machinery, with the aid of the nerves and ganglions, to execute all the involuntary functions of the body. Its offices are numerous and its work perpetual. The contraction of a muscle is by direct application of electricity; the relaxation, by a suspension of that application, which requires a cut-off or disconnection. All voluntary movements require this peculiar function used in telegraphing. The involuntary motions of the heart seem to require a double-geared connection, by means of which the auricles contract when the ventricles expand and vice versa. This connection between the brain battery and the conducting nerves is hard to find, but it exists all the same. The loss of power to disconnect causes the disease called shaking palsy. There is a constant leakage of the electric fluid upon the voluntary nerves and muscles that causes the shaking. There is no paralysis about it unless it is of that little motor brain that forms the connection. Paralysis is a suspension of function, a cessation of electric effect. This may be produced by derangement of a portion of the battery, or of the nerves, in such a manner that the fluid does not reach its destination, or by a diseased condition of the organ to be moved by it. When a wound is made in the flesh, a bone broken, or an obstruction of function produced, the dictates of the cerebellum sends to the seat of damage an unusual quantity of electricity, for the purpose of repairs, which collects from the blood the formative elements of tissue, and builds them into the lesion as a bricklayer repairs a damaged wall.

Strychnine, the alkaloid of nux vomica, is one of the most active poisons in use, yet very few persons know how death is produced by it so suddenly. It is either a powerful generative of electricity, or it connects the battery with the system in such a manner that the muscular structure is contracted so tightly that the heart cannot open to receive and transmit the blood. More clearly it produces spasmodic contraction of the heart, arteries and veins, by an extraordinary flow of electricity upon the circulatory organs, so completely suspending their functions that death is the immediate result. To know the effects caused by strychnia should suggest its use in certain cases of general debility or partial electric exhaustion. It may be used in minute doses, but nux vomica is much safer.

Morphia, an alkaloid of opium, is the opposite of strychnia. It is a narcotic. It is claimed to allay morbid sensibility, relieve pain and produce sleep—also coma, convulsions and death. Morphine possesses no recuperative or curative properties as a medicine. It produces a suspension of electric force by disqualifying the brain to produce it or the nerves to transmit it. Or it destroys, expels or exhausts it in the system so the knowledge of an injury going on in the body cannot be conveyed to the brain. The wound is becoming more malignant, the pain continues, but the messenger cannot report the condition to headquarters The work of destruction and disorganization go on the same, though the patient does not know it. It produces sleep. It makes no difference whether exhaustion is produced by long continued fatigue or by morphine, sleep will come to the relief of the unfortunate victim the same.

Medical men frequently ride hobbies and follow the dogmas of their predecessors with as much zeal and as little original investigation, as the political masses follow the names of their parties. Once established upon a false hypothesis, the reasoning, treatment and results are all a failure. Morphine is the greatest enemy of mankind that lurks on the shelves of the druggist, not excepting calomel, which is a universal solvent of the blood, muscular tissues and bone.

Is light something or nothing? According to a theory now partially accepted, it is a form of motion, and called the undulatory theory. "It is supposed that there exists throughout all space an etheral, elastic fluid which, like the air, is capable of receiving and transmitting undulations or vibrations. These, reaching the eye, affect the optic nerve and produce the sensation which we call light. According to this theory, there is a striking analogy between the eye and the ear."

I do not accept this theory for several reasons. There is no proof that such an ether exists in all space; it is supposed to exist. There is no proof that it vibrates to the right and left, or at right angles to its line of motion, for it cannot be seen, heard, felt, tasted, smelt, weighed, measured or tested by instruments. There is no analogy in the structure of the eye and ear that could give to the former any of the properties or qualities for receiving vibrations which the latter possesses. The ear, which is made to receive impressions from the vibrations of air, presents a large concave surface to the traveling wave, to gather a liberal quantity of the fluid into a funnel-shaped tube leading into the head about one inch, where the outer drumhead is drawn across the tube and called the membrane of the tympanum or drum of the ear. A short distance beyond the first drum is a second membrane across the tube, forming the air cavity of the real drum, which is ventilated by a tube called the eustachian tube, which opens out into the back part of the mouth. The two drumheads are connected by a chain of four small bones, attached to the center of each membrane. Beyond the drum is the real ear, called the labyrinth, which is a cavity in a hard bone. The parts consist of a vestibule, three semicircular canals, a winding cavity called the cochlea, across which about three thousand nerve strings of different length are drawn like harp strings. The whole cavity is filled with a fluid in which the nerves are submerged. When the outer drum is jarred or vibrated by a wave of atmosphere, that vibration is communicated by the chain of bones to the inner membrane and the fluid of the lyra. Each string will vibrate its own corresponding sound or vibration, in volume, length, pitch and tone, which is reported by the auditory nerve to the seat of knowledge.

Human eyes consist of two hollow globes, about one inch in diameter, consisting essentially of four coats which form the outer wall, except at the entrance of the optic nerve, and a window in front called the cornea. It contains three cavities filled with transparent liquids, called aqueous, crystalline and vitrious humors. The optic nerve enters at the back part of the eye, where it expands and forms the inner coat of the eye. The point of expansion is called the retina, or seat of vision. The crystalline fluid is encased in a sack having the form of a double convex lens, and is located near the front part of the eye. Light is emitted from a luminous body and thrown from a reflecting surface in straight rays or lines. Several rays are called a beam of light. Rays of light reflected from an object and entering the eye are refracted by the cornea and crystalline lens and conveyed to a focus, so as to form an image or shadow of the object on the retina. The impress of this shadow upon the seat of vision produces the sense of sight, which is reported by the optic nerve to the seat of knowledge.

If any person can see any analogy between a harp and a photograph, he can see more than I can. Suppose we subject the drum of the ear to a thousand sounds or vibrations of atmosphere at once, ranging from the heaviest clap of thunder to the finest chirp of the cricket—how many distinct, intelligent sounds would the listener get? Bring a thousand stars in range of the pupil of the eye, and each will be photographed upon the retina individually. If vibration produces the images of objects, why would not such a multitude of waves mingle, mix and blend the whole into one confused mass of light? Sound waves blend into perfect confusion. Why would not light waves do the same? Again, the undulatory theory destroys all color in solar light as seen in the spectrum, and claims it is all in your eye! Instead of saying light from the sun contains seven distinct colors, this theory says a wave of ether from the sun contains seven distinct waves of unequal vibrations! The red wave vibrates 39,000 times in one inch of space, and 474,000,000,000 times in one second of time. When this wave strikes the cornea, jarring the ether in the aqueous, crystalline and vitrious humors of the eye, then the optic nerve feels red! The violet wave, which is the other extreme of the spectrum, vibrates 57,500 times in one inch, and 699,000,000,000 times in a second. This wave makes the nerve feel violet! Now, when the waves are all traveling in company in the form of white light, at whose rate of motion do they move? Whose music do they march to? If each marches to his own time, each would show his own color. But if all get down to the red, slow movement when in company, what motor power gives them a new and different impetus as soon as they pass through a prism and are reflected back from the spectrum to the eye? How easily the phenomena of nature can be understood and explained, when it is known that electricity is composed of fluid matter containing every feasible atom on the surface of the sun, which is transmitted directly from that central mass to all his planet children, replacing all the solidified elements, not excepting that wonderful carbonic acid gas, which is supposed by recent progressive philosophers to be replenished from ether occupying the inter-planetary spaces.

I have just been favored with a synopsis of the twelfth and closing lecture of Prof. Langley, of Allegheny Observatory, delivered at Lowell Institute. Theme: "The wonders of the sky;" "Comets and meteors the waste of worlds." The professor appears to be wonderfully puzzled on the formation and phenomena of comets and meteors. He thinks "the fact that the comet's tail is uniformly pushed away from the sun demonstrates that, in spite of the prevalent belief that the solar influence is one of attraction as seen in gravitation, it has in some way a repellant force." The world does move! Holding what he declared to be a piece of comet in his hand, the speaker said, "It had a history more thrilling than that of any atom of our earth, if it could only tell its story." "So that it appears, in short, that meteors and comets are portions of demolished, worn out worlds." "It is manifest, then, that these meteors come from a world much like our own." "Is this the end?" These few short quotations show the false conclusions that are certain to follow a false hypothesis. Pope better understood the order of nature in his day. He says:

> "From nature's chain whatever link you strike,
> Tenth or ten thousandth, breaks the chain alike.
> And, if each system in gradation roll,
> Alike essential to the amazing whole.
> The least confusion but in one, not all
> That system only, but the whole, must fall.
> Let earth unbalanced from her orbit fly,
> Planets and suns (comets) run lawless thro' the sky;
> Let ruling angels from their spheres be hurled,
> Being on being wrecked, and world on world—
> All this dread ORDER break—for whom? for thee?
> Vile worm! Oh, madness! pride! impiety!

The professor says: "From all our varied studies we learn that this present universe is the successor of those that preceded it, and is but the predecessor of those to come after." If he had said planetary systems, it would be all right. Again: "All our studies lead us to be careful of presumptuous speculations." All my studies lead me to guard against stupid traditions. If vibrations of ether are light, where do the heat and chemical rays come from? Electricity is the great agent of light, heat, motion and attraction.

D. W. ELDERKIN.

Spartansburg, Pa., April 28th, 1883.

ELECTRICITY.

The world parts with old theories with great reluctance, and receives new ones tardily. These theories will meet with opposition and possibly with ridicule, but they are no less likely to contain some truth on that account.

Electricity is the great soul of the universe; this expression does not mean that electricity is the Deity, but that it is the great agent or source of light, heat, motion and attraction.

It produces all the motions and regulates all the functions by which the animal economy is carried on. The brain is an electrical apparatus consisting of two separate and distinct apartments, called the cerebrum and cerebellum — the former the anterior and superior portion of the brain, and the latter the inferior and posterior part of it. The body is ramified with small, delicate white cords, called nerves, which are named ganglionic, sympathetic and cerebro-spinal. The last is divided into sensitive and motor nerves. These are connected to the brain by the means of the spinal cord and the medulla oblongata. Motor nerves are those used to produce voluntary motion. They are covered from their origin to the muscle in which they terminate with a sheath which is believed to be a non-conductor of electricity. That part of the nerve which enters the muscle is destitute of the sheath, leaving the current of electricity free to diffuse itself through the muscle.

A muscle is a bundle of fibres enclosed in a thin cellular membrane, and attached at the head end to a superior bone. It is large in the middle, tapering down toward the tail, where it changes its red color to white, forming a tendon, which is inserted into an inferior bone below the joint. The fibres or threads of a muscle are made up of a series of rings extending from one end to the other. When we desire to contract a muscle and thereby move a limb or a member of our body, the organ of firmness in the cerebrum, located near the crown of the head, applies a current of electricity to the nerve which is connected to the muscle inserted into the part to be moved. The electricity, flowing upon the rings of the fibres, expands their circumference, thereby rendering them thinner longitudinally, and consequently shorter, causing the point of insertion to move toward the point of attachment. Thus we raise our arm, crook our finger, or shut our eye. Great electrical shocks in our system are from the cerebral battery.

When the blood flows to the brain in uniform healthy quantities, the governor has complete control of his battery; but when, from cordiac or arterial debility or other cause, the brain is emptied of blood, the person faints or falls down with an epileptic fit. A horizontal position will restore the equilibrium in case of syncope and relieve the symptom. But in epilepsy greater effort is required. The whole charge of the cerebral battery is thrown upon the motor nerves simultaneously, causing every muscle of voluntary motion to contract at the same time. The stronger muscles to a great extent predominate over the weaker. The head and shoulders are bent back, the arms and hands inward, and the legs backward with a winding, twisting, vermicular movement, producing the contortions and clonic spasms manifested in the falling sickness. The tension produced upon the muscular system by such a shock of electric energy appears to be nature's own method of forcing the blood from the extremities to the head again. A state of stupor or insensibility with slumber follows such a fit usually before consciousness is restored. Sleep appears to be the great medium through which the electric energy of the brain is restored. Great physical force is produced by a corresponding quantity of electricity expended upon the muscles. Respiration as well as sleep appears to be a means of replenishing the brain, for during slumber the breathing is longer and stronger than when awake, and when rapid motions are continued, which require large expenditures of electricity, the breathing is increased in proportion.

Chemical action carried on in the process of digestion and mechanical friction caused by the circulation of the blood probably generates electricity.

The base brain contains the intelligence and machinery, with the aid of the ganglions, to execute all the involuntary functions of the body. Its offices are numerous and its work perpetual. How its electric current can be thrown upon the muscles of the heart alternately in such a manner that when the auricles contract the ventricles expand and vice versa, is a question that has occupied my mind long and anxious hours.

The contraction of a muscle is by direct electric application; the relaxation by a suspension of that application which requires a cut off or disconnection. It would seem that this must be done at or near the plexus. The cerebellum appears to contain a silent, unknown partner of the conscious man, who manipulates all the healing process of the body. If this part of the brain is large, its possessor has a promise of long life, great endurance and enviable health; but if small, his years are few and liable to pain and debility.

The brain not only furnishes electric fluid for the operations of all the other parts of the system, but it furnishes itself with electric motor power by means of which the sensations we call thought are produced. The folds of the brain are movable and susceptible of an innumerable number of changes by contractions, expansions, involutions, evolutions and contortions. When we learn *one* thing, it is done training the brain to perform *one* movement till it becomes habitual to that movement. When we have learned many things the brain has been trained to make as many movements. These maneuvers, in classes, become associated in such a manner as to produce what we designate as ideas. Memory consists in the retentive power of the brain to produce its trained movements of earlier days. The man who carries a hundred thousand trained changes in his brain will find it much more difficult to reproduce a long neglected evolution or thought tnan the person who carries only one thousand. By this we infer that the less a person knows the better he can remember it. A portion of the scientific world call the electricity of the human body *nervous fluid.* Why may we not as well call the electricity used in telegraphing metallic fluid, or that falling from a cloud nimbic fluid, or that excited from a cat's back feline fluid? If we know the brain is a battery, the nerves the conductors, and the fluid electricity, may we not better understand what is meant by *nervous debility* and how to restore nervous energy? The nerves may be in a state of health, and the brain not sufficiently charged with electricity to impart suitable energy to the heart, liver, kidneys, muscles, glands, capillaries and ducts to work them up to the standard of health. In this situation the person's condition is better represented by the phrase, electric exhaustion, than by nervous debility. Paralysis is a suspension of function, a cessation of electric effect. This may be produced by derangement of a portion of the battery, or of the nerve in such a manner that the fluid does not reach its destination, or by a diseased condition of the organ to be moved by it. We must know the how and the where and the which, what and when before our prescriptions will cure all the diseases of men.

When a wound is made in the flesh, a bone broken or an obstruction of function produced, the dictates of the cerebellum sends to the seat of damage an unusual force of electric energy for the purpose of repairs, which collects from the blood the formative elements of tissue, and builds them into the lesion as a bricklayer repairs a broken wall. This accumulation of electric energy and material exhibit the symptoms we call inflammation. People are often unnecessarily frightened about slight indications of inflammation. A surgeon, to avoid inflammation, once kept a wounded foot saturated with ice water till it died and had to be amputated.

Morphine possesses no curative properties as a medicine. It produces a suspension of electric force by disqualifying the brain to produce it or the nerves to transmit it. As all curative processes are carried on through the agency of electric energy, a suspension, or partial obstruction of that agent retards the healing process in the same ratio. The sleep induced by it is the unconscious slumber of an epileptic fit. In cases of burns, scalds, cancers, etc., when the suffering is intolerable, and there is no hope of recovery, it is an act of kindness to produce a state of partial insensibility by the use of morphine.

When external force comes in contact with any part of the body, the agitation produced among the molecules liberates a quantity of latent electricity, which is taken up by the nerves of sensation and transmitted to the brain, where the dispatch is received, and we are made conscious of any lesion produced in that locality.

The above is only a few bungling illustrations of the influence exerted by electricity over the condition and life of man.

D. W. ELDERKIN.

May 15th, 1885.

ARE THESE THINGS SO, AND WHY?

It has been said for at least eighteen hundred years, that when the clouds are red in the west it will be a fair day to-morrow. There is some truth in this old adage. Our rain storms come mostly from the west, the clouds moving toward the east. When the western edge appears above the horizon, the sky being clear between it and the setting sun, the cloud acts as a prism, separating the red rays of light from the others and refracting them to the eye of the observer, which gives us the red cloud in the west. During the night the great sheet of cloud moves forward east, leaving us in the long space of clear sky west of the cloud. If no other influence ever interfered with this condition we could be certain of a clear day to-morrow every time the clouds are red in the west at sun set. But clouds may be driven into this clear streak of sky from the north or south, and take up their line of march in the same direction of their file-leader and give us a shower the next day in spite of the observations of the Jews.

Why does the wind blow from the west more than from the east? The east side of the earth or the side toward the sun has continual day, which is warmer than the west or night side. The cool night opens into day at its eastern edge where the atmosphere is warmer and rarified by the heat of the sun, causing it to rise, when the cool air from the night side rushes forward, eastward, toward the opening day to equalize the vacuum, causing the wind to blow in that direction.

Why is it said where the moon runs high it will be cold and dry? The attractive influence of the moon acts the same upon the atmosphere of the earth as upon the water, causing tides. With this variation the tides of the air are enormously high, and extend over a vast territory of country in a circular form, resembling a caldron kettle turned bottom-side up. When the moon is high in the northern hemisphere it may be 28 1-7° north of the equator. It then draws a large portion of its vast tide from the cold regions of the north, where the atmosphere is lightly impregnated with water, causing our winds to be cold and dry. As the moon falls back toward the south, by a certain retrograde movement it loses its attractive power at the north and draws more strongly upon the warm and wet air of the tropical regions, giving us warm breezes and abundant showers. When the moon is high it is nearly in range with the setting sun on first appearance of the new moon. The light streak we see is the lower edge of that side which faces the sun, and we say the moon lays on its back; that is, its south point is nearly as high as the north end. This is called a dry moon. But when it is low in the south, the angle of vision is changed so we see further under the northwest side, giving the north end of the light streak an elevated appearance, while the southwest side is hidden from view, giving it the appearance of a steep slope downward. This is called the wet moon. These changes in the horns of the moon indicate its location or its relative position to the sun and the observer, and publish alike to the philosopher and the heathen: "I am high, cold and dry, or low, warm and wet."

The idea that the four changes of the moon, as noted in almanacs, mark fixed periods for change of weather, is all an uneducated old man's whim. One observer marked the changes of moon and weather during a period of three years and found one more storm half-way between the changes than occurred at the changes. The moon changes every day, hour and minute.

A great majority of the people of this enlightened and refined age believe that the twelve signs of the zodiac pass through a person's body, from head to foot, once every lunar month. They are so positive of it that a thousand witnesses could be found in a short time who would swear to horrid results they have been eye-witnesses to, where certain things have been done when the sign or the twelve signs of the zodiac were in the heart. It is understood that when a child is weaned with the signs in the heart, that there is no way to get rid of them only to work them off through the bowels, which causes irritation, restlessness, starting and screaching out in its sleep. Well, it is no use to argue this question, for the old people who have raised families have all seen children have these symptoms, and more, even looseness of the bowels at the same time, when there was no reason for it, only the poor thing was taken off from its dinner when the signs were in the heart, or the bowels, which is just as bad.

D. W. ELDERKIN.

Spartansburg, Pa., June 20th, 1883.

WHAT IS A MAGNETIC NEEDLE;

AND WHY DOES IT TURN ITS NEGATIVE END TOWARD THE NORTH POLE?

These questions have not been answered satisfactorily to profound thinkers. It is known that a certain ore of iron, sometimes called lodestone, is a magnet that will communicate an influence to a steel bar which will, when suspended, cause one end to turn nearly in the direction of the north pole, while the other end points nearly south.

But what is this magnet, and what is the influence communicated to the steel needle? I call it a peculiar kind of condensed electricity, which, when applied to a piece of steel, charges it positively at one end and negatively at the other.

It has been supposed that a large mass of lodestone or magnetic oxide of iron exists about 19½° south of the north pole in the direction of Hudson's Bay; and that to this positive point of attraction the negative end of the needle is drawn.

If that theory is true, the needle would point invariably in that direction from every place in the northern hemisphere, which is not a fact.

It may well be doubted whether there is any such point of central attraction, while it is admitted that there is a general tendency in the needle to point in that direction. Can we find any other influence besides attraction that can and does influence the magnetic needle so as to determine the direction it will point? It is known that two positively charged bodies repel each other.

A current of positive electricity passing under a magnetic needle repels the positive end of it, and drives it as far from the electric wire as it can go, causing the needle to stand at right angle to the conducting wire. This fact, as demonstrated by Prof. Oersted, shows conclusively that a current of electricity traveling under a compass will determine the direction the needle will point.

Now, let us for a moment examine the currents of electricity at the surface of the earth, and ascertain, if possible, how and where they originate, and in what direction they move, and how they will affect the compass. Hot bodies are positively or actively electrified; cold ones are comparatively negative, which causes a current to travel from the positive to the negative. The tropical regions of our earth evolve electricity, which, if not otherwise controlled, would move in straight lines from the equator to the poles. But this it does not do. It starts from the hot or day side of the earth, and moves toward the morning edge of the night side—that is, it travels from the noon meridian toward the morning meridian, which gives it a western course which just keeps pace with the earth's revolution on its axis. Day constantly chases night westward, always firing its electric volleys into night's cold edge. This movement of electricity is not directly west, but appears to follow the lines of temperature. If the land surface of the northern hemisphere had been equally distributed around the pole with uniform elevation and temperature the helix of this electric current would wind up or center exactly at the pole. In that case the magnetic needle, standing at right angle with the electric current, would uniformly point to the north pole from every place in north latitude. But the temperature of different parts of the earth in the same latitude being greatly unequal, the regularity of the electric current is very materially disturbed, by variations to the north and south, as the land surface is more or less elevated or depressed. The current may be weakened by actual absorption of the electricity into high, cold, mountainous regions, while it would retain its volume in low, warm sections. Such is the elevation of the northern part of the western continent above the eastern, that the helix or center of motion of the diurnal electric currents is wound up 19½° south of the pole in the direction of Hudson's Bay. If we take a great pair of imaginary compasses and place one point in what is called the center of attraction, but what I call the center of electric motion, near Hudson's Bay, and swing the other point over the pole 19½° into Siberia and around to, and across, the continent of America 39° south of the pole, we will have the general average of the course of the current around the northern hemisphere. The compass varies at Boston 5½° west, at Greenland 50° west, in England 24° west, and at St. Petersburg 6° west.

It is said there are two lines, called the eastern and western lines of no variation, where the needle points directly to the north pole. The western line begins at 60° north latitude, west of Hudson's Bay; thence south, bearing to the east, through Lake Michigan down the great valley of the Mississippi, across the Gulf of Mexico, to the eastern point of South America. In moving south about 60°, this line varies to the east about 42°. The eastern line begins about 66° north latitude in the White Sea, makes a great semicircular sweep easterly till it reaches the latitude of 71° north, then passes down the Sea of Japan, goes westward across China and Hindostan to Bombay, then bends east, touches Australia and goes south. This line runs north 5° and east 100°, then south 16°, and west 70°, then southeast to Australia.

Now, upon the hypothesis that there is a great mass of toxide of iron near Hudson's Bay, toward which the magnetic needle is invariably drawn, there can be only two lines on which the needle will point to the pole. The western line must begin at the south side of this center of attraction and run a direct south course; the eastern line must begin at the pole, 180° east of the other line, and run south. There could be no variation east or west of these lines, and have a center of attraction located 19½° from the pole, and yet attract to the pole. Place your compass where you please on these lines, and the needle would always be true to the north pole. But the needle placed on these true north and south lines does not point to the north pole. What then becomes of the theory of a center of attraction? It has gone with Moses' history of the creation of the world. By traveling down the western line of no variation of compass we will find the line itself varies so as to cross sections of country where the temperature is even, its line of change varying north and south, while east and west the temperature is equal on the same latitude. The eastern line is much more circuitous, wandering out on the low northern lands of Siberia, down into China, thence westward through a country of even temperature, avoiding mountains and currents of cold winds, to find sections where the temperature runs in straight lines east and west.

By referring to the lines of temperature in our rocky mountain territories, we find almost an indescribable amount of irregularity. In the same locality the common magnetic compass varies so greatly that its use is abandoned and the solar compass introduced for all official business. Thus we find there is only a general tendency of the needle to point to the center of the electric helix, attended with all the variations that the lines of temperature and currents of electricity are subjected to. It is said by mariners that the further north they sail the more feeble is the action of the compass. At 72° north the compass will not indicate its polarity without frequent shaking. This fact shows that the greater the degree of cold, the weaker the electric current, and the less power to repel the needle to a right angular position.

But how does this feeble action of the needle comport

with the theory of a great mountain of lodestone? The nearer you approach an attractive power, the stronger the attraction. This is known to be true in magnetism.

Let us review this theory and see if we understand it. Magnetism is a kind of condensed electricity that adheres to steel for a great length of time. It is positive and repulsive to other kinds of electricity—will cause a magnetic needle to stand at right angle to the line of motion of a strong current of electricity passing under it. The heat of the sun on the day side of the earth evolves electricity, which moves westward toward the cold edge of the night side of the world. This current of electricity is strongest directly under the sun from tropic to tropic, and grows weaker constantly toward the poles. It is governed in its western movement by the lines of temperature. That, where the lines of temperature run even or equal east and west, the electric current runs directly west, and the needle, standing at right angle to the current, will point due north. Wherever the current is influenced to the northwest or southwest, the needle will vary accordingly. This great sheet of electricity, in its diurnal course around the earth, is carried 19½° nearer the pole on the eastern continent than on the western. This variation is caused by the low lands of Asia and the high mountains of America.

The center of motion from these causes is located 19½° from the pole. The theory of a center of attraction is false, as shown by the two true north and south lines, as well as by the two wandering lines, which can vary from 42° to 100° from the range of attraction, and yet pull up straight to the north pole. As you approach the electric helix, the action upon the needle is weakened. If it is a magnet pile, the nearer you approach it, the stronger the attraction.

D. W. ELDERKIN.

Spartansburg, Pa., 1884.

PRODUCING SHOWERS OF RAIN.

Nature's method of watering the land surface of this earth, when carefully scrutinized, exhibits to the mind of man a wonderful display of combination and change. Our globe is surrounded by a very light, elastic, movable atmosphere, composed principally of oxygen and nitrogen gases, which extend upward forty or fifty miles and has a weight or pressure at the surface of the earth of fifteen pounds to the square inch. It is set in motion by heat, attraction of the moon and electricity, in such a manner as to move at different times in every possible direction. This atmosphere, though vastly lighter than water, is used as a vehicle to buoy up and carry away floods of water over the dry land. The evaporating stratum of the atmosphere extends from one to three miles in highth. Above this is a lighter, and the rain forming stratum. Water, which is so essential to animal and vegetable life, is composed of oxygen and hydrogen gases, so combined that heat and motion separate and rarify them till they are lighter than the evaporating stratum of the air, through which they rise to the rain-forming or cloud-floating stratum. In the lower portion of this stratum they are condensed into clouds, mists and showers, which are poured down upon the thirsty earth to renew and invigorate its vital powers. A portion of it is absorbed into the earth, whence it makes its way to the surface again in the form of springs for constant use. The regularity of the distribution is not so complete that every portion of the land surface is always supplied with sufficient water to insure the complete growth and maturity of vegetation; hence large sections of country often suffer severely from drought. Has man power to interfere, so as to direct or control the laws of nature to his use and advantage? He most certainly has, just in proportion to his knowledge. Electricity has been subjugated to the uses of the telegraph, telephone and electric lights. Fire and water have been made to generate a locomotive power that is almost unlimited. By the combination of simple, harmless materials, explosives are produced that defy the cohesive powers of nature. Would not infinite knowledge give to man unlimited power over the laws of nature?

For the purpose of producing a shower during a drouth, Nathaniel Cary and your humble correspondent drew out a plan of operations as follows, viz: Erect in any valuable locality a central office, provided with implements for testing the amount of moisture in the atmosphere, a telegraph and telephone, with a large mortar so arranged that it could be loaded and fired upward in rapid succession. On a circle whose radius is five miles from the central office, arrange fifteen mortars at equal distance from each other, to be fired by an electric spark from the central office. When conditions are favorable, signs of rain appear which usually fail in a dry time; let the chief call his gunners to their posts, when they may fire from twenty to forty rounds, as may be found necessary by experience.

The sound waves will expand horizontally and perpendicularly, meeting, cutting and elevating each other, by means of which the whole atmosphere over an area of four hundred square miles will become agitated and rarified. This condition of the evaporating stratum will permit the mists and clouds to settle down into it, where condensation will take place by the superior weight of the lower stratum when it assumes its usual condition. We believe this simple process would force the heavens to give us a shower, when without it we might be scorched for two or three weeks. The experiment might be made by our national government with an outlay of but a few thousand dollars. One good shower over the gardening district of Philadelphia in a drouth would be worth millions of dollars.

Such batteries arranged over the State of Kansas and other Western States and Territories subject to drouth might be worth more than all the gold mines of California. Cyclones and electric hurricanes or tornadoes may be reduced by these batteries. It is also possible that eggs and larva of insects may be destroyed by the thunders of this rain producer.

I invite a careful scientific investigation of this subject.

A few years ago we addressed this plan of operation, with appropriate drawings, to our member of Congress, who was so unscientific that he received it as a drive, a bore on himself, and never presented it that we know of; he utterly refused to answer any letters in regard to it.

We presented the subject in the form of a petition, signed by all the intellectual members of our community, asking Congress to test it by appropriate appliances, under the guidance of talent adapted to the work. No one heard of our plan outside of the vicinity of Spartansburg. Friend Carey is dead, and I am sixty-six years on the road toward my long home, and I want this theory ventilated. It may make fruitful fields "where naught but arid waste is found."

D. W. Elderkin.

Spartansburg, Pa., December 4th, 1883.

FINANCIAL.

Much is said in regard to the action of Congress on the financial question. What will that body do? What ought it to do? Better do nothing than something wrong. Never was there a time when it was more important to act wisely than the present. If a financial crash is brought on within the next four years the Republican party will crash with it, for the mass of our laboring and voting populace do not understand financial matters; but they do understand the difference between two dollars or a bushel of potatoes for a day's work. They can realize a distinction between paying for a living and getting in debt for it and being sold out by the sheriff. Wealthy speculators bring on a financial panic that they may become richer while the poor become poorer. Legislation should take care of the laboring poor.

There is a great cry from a few bond-holders for the Government to resume specie payment. Where is the gold with which to resume specie payment? and to what extent in the abyss of bankruptcy must we descend to reach it within the next four years? If gold is what we have the least of, and what we want most why not raise our tariff scale to that point which will produce the greatest amount of revenue, and at the same time prevent so large an amount of specie going out of the country on account of balance of trade against us? And why not use this specie each year so far as it will go to cancel our pressing liabilities, and supply the deficiency, when necessary, by renewed promises to pay. The people have a great national debt. Their ability to pay depends upon the amount of money they have. This debt was mostly created when a small quantity of beef demanded a large amount of government obligations. Now if Congress should enact resumption within one year, the scale would be reversed and a large amount of property would command only a small amount of money, diminishing the ability of the people to pay in the same ratio that their property would be decreased in value. Resumption of specie payment implies a reduction of paper circulation, because the amount of paper so greatly exceeds the specie in our country that the government and banks issuing it could not meet the demands of the hungry gold idolators. This state of the currency would produce a panic that would run gold from its present rate up to one hundred or one hundred and fifty per cent., if it did not produce bankruptcy throughout the entire country. But if it were possible to resume at the present time it would be highly impolitic and unjust.

The bond-holders who are already reaping a rich harvest from the people would have their bonds enhanced in value in the same proportion that the producer's property would be diminished in value, because the value of money depends upon the amount of property it will purchase. Decrease the quantity and you increase the quality or value. Decrease the ability of the people to pay and you increase the debt they owe at the same rate. If our national debt is $2,500,-000,000, then on the scale of population each individual owes about $70. When winter is passed a good cow will bring the same amount. The person who can spare such a cow or the equivalent in other property can pay his share of the national liabilities. But if we resume specie payment and thereby contract the currency one half, then it would require two cows to pay the $70, which is in effect doubling his debt by requiring him to work twice as long to produce twice as much property as is required at present rates. We may as well raise our national debt to $5,000,000,000 as to require the people to pay $2,500,000,000 when property will bring only one-half what it now sells for.

What, then, ought Congress to do financially? Simply hold money matters steady by fixing the time of specie resumption at least ten years in the future. This will enable the people North and South to recover from the shock of war and pay their debt incurred by drafts and bounties and the absence of husbands and sons whose labors were necessary to keep up family expenses.

Some people think nothing can be money only what will chink. A little further investigation shows that anything may be used for money that is or can be made scarce, easy to be transported, and convenient for exchange. A gold basis has nothing to do in determining the value of a dollar. If we had gold enough to give each person in the United States ten dollars, with no other circulating medium, and which would bring wheat at one dollar per bushel, double the amount of gold for each one and wheat would bring two dollars per bushel. So a gold dollar would be worth only half as much as in the first supposition. Then it is not the kind of money that makes its value, but the quantity or scarcity.

The specie advocate says without gold, how would you redeem any other currency? I answer, how can you redeem specie? When gold is worn and obliterated so it will no longer pass, government shaves it as much as the loss in weight and gives you new pieces of the same material.

If you had money, the value of which does not depend upon its weight or size, but upon its device and stamp, then government can give you a new dollar for the old one without shave and thus redeem it.

D. W. ELDERKIN.

Spartansburg, Pa., 1867.

OUR LEGISLATURE.

The summer, with its multiplicity of labor and care is passed. Our crops of hay and grain for the coming year, with butter, cheese, fruit and vegetables are produced. Mechanics have, in a measure, completed their jobs, and mariners returned to their homes to enjoy the blessings of family and society. Individual enterprise is thus partially suspended, leaving the mind free to look abroad to examine our collective interests and future welfare.

As citizens of Pennsylvania we all make up one great community, or family, whose legal rights are delegated to a Legislature which, under the Federal Congress, enacts all the laws, rules and regulations, directly or indirectly, that govern this great family. I say *govern;* I mean more than is commonly understood or expressed by that term. Law has something to do with every individual in every period of his life, from the cradle to the grave. It makes his birth and relation to his parents legitimate or illegitimate. It directs and forms, in a degree, his religious, moral and intellectual education. It establishes his right of property, both personal and real, and, in a general sense, controls his person, disposes of his estate, and holds his life in keeping for the common good of all.

Looking with an eye of scrutiny upon the all-controlling and disposing powei of *Law*, a person may judge, though imperfectly, of the vast amount of good secured by equal and just legislation, while language would fail to describe, though the tongue were inspired with liquid flames of utterance, the irremediable wrongs, calamities and ruin that follow weak, unwise and partial law making.

Effecting the weal or woe of such a multitude of human beings, how important it is that our laws should secure equal advantage and facilities to all classes, and be so clear from complication, intricacies and apparent contradictions, that the masses of the people can understand them.

That they may be such, it becomes necessary that our statutes should be frequently revised by removing those acts, sections and clauses which, by subsequent legislation, have been repealed. Those remaining on the statute books, interspersed and commingled with those portions that are still in force, render our laws as incomprehensible to the common people as the edicts of Nero, posted on steeples and towers so high that his subjects could not read them.

Purdon's Digest is the standard work on statute law, and yet it is believed that two-thirds of that book is repealed flood trash. In acts not repealed as whole, sections or clauses, and certain words or lines are struck out, certain parts of sections and acts added, which repeal all laws to the contrary notwithstanding. To show that a common man can see the point in law as clear as mud, I will illustrate by supposing an act approved the 27th day of March, 1868, amending an act passed 1855, to consolidate certain acts passed 1812, relating to acts of 1801, regulating the statutes of King George and Queen Elizabeth in regard to treason, felony and other high crimes and misdemeanors.

Four years ago, by act of our Legislature, three eminent judges were appointed to revise our laws by clearing out all the superfluous stale, torpid, inert, repealed portions, and to present to the Legislature and the people the real letter and spirit of the law, in a condensed form, so that all the acts pertaining to one subject would be condensed into one. I understand the work was about completed over one year ago and presented to the Legislature for examination, amendment and sanction.

For reasons unknown to the people that work was not

done. A feeling of disappointment and dissatisfaction is manifested all through this great family. Some say perhaps our representatives mistake themselves for our lords instead of our honored servants. Some think our legal gentlemen derive large revenues from litigation arising out of complexity of the law; while others say our members can make more stamps by selling the people's time and their own talents to some moneyed monopolies than they can to do the work their constituents sent them to do. This kind of whining and grumbling amounts to nothing. Our Legislature is what we make it as to material, and what we allow it to be in character.

If we feel a necessity for a revision of our laws let us speak out in language that will be understood. If we, the people, cannot speak for ourselves, let us ask the press, the guardian of the people's liberties, to speak for us. Let us call upon our learned judges and the legal profession to speak for us and to do justice by us.

We are tired of so much special and local legislation. We are tired of seeing each year a pamphlet of six hundred pages of legislation in which the great laboring population have no interest except to know how much their present liberties are curtailed. Whether their cows can or cannot be turned into the road to drink; whether they can or cannot sell their rags, old iron and sheep pelts for tin pails and pans, or whether they can sell one-half of a sheep or hog the same as a whole one without being liable to fine and imprisonment.

It appears to us that the greater the amount of natural liberty that a people can enjoy without infringing upon the life, liberty, property or character of others, the better it is for them as a whole. Laws may become so multifarious in form, complex in character, partial in structure and numerous in restrictions, that, instead of being a protection of the people's liberties, they form a net work around them, binding them hand an foot, and reducing them to a state of hopeless serfdom.

Will our Legislature reduce the quantity and increase the quality of our laws?

Will our Legislature give us general laws, instead of special acts favoring particular persons and localities? Will they begin the work this winter?

Say, people, say! Answer, Leislature, answer!

D. W. ELDERKIN.

1868.

CONSUMPTION.

A NEW THEORY OF THE ORIGIN, PROGRESS AND CURE OF PULMONARY CONSUMPTION.

My theory is that this much-dreaded disease commences at the external integument, either from direct cause or by imperfect hereditary formation. The excretory ducts of the sebaceous glands become closed, shutting off from the surface their lubricating oil, causing the skin to dry and shrink to such an extent that the sweat pores and mouths of the lymphatics are closed. This condition produces derangement of the system in three different directions. First, the effete matter that should be thrown off through the pores by exudation, or imperceptible perspiration, is entirely closed in at the surface, causing a violent electric effort to force the passage through the skin. This effort of the human battery generates an unnatural heat all over the body, which slowly but certainly consumes the tissues and wastes the recuperative powers of life. This rejected matter failing to escape through its natural channel, is taken up by the blood and carried upon and through the thoracic and abdominal viscera, where its deleterious effects are exhibited more clearly by irritation of the lungs, derangement of the liver and debility of the stomach.

The second great injury is produced by impairing the respiratory functions of the skin. It is well known to physiologists that a person can live but a short time if the atmosphere is entirely excluded from the skin, and also if a large area of the surface of the body is scalded, death is certain.

Yet the fact that the skin breathes or inhales oxygen from the surrounding atmosphere has never, within my knowledge, been mentioned by pathological writers; and from their mode of treating consumptives, one would naturally conclude they never knew anything about it; and from the universal fatality of the disease, that they cared nothing about it.

In the minute circulatory vessels of the skin, where the blood moves slowly, it is positively essential to life that oxygenation is affected directly through the integument. The third injury arises from extravasation of the sebaceous fluid, which resembles lard, though more of a glutinous nature, which, when forced through the walls of the sebaceous cups, is taken up by the blood and carried into the lungs, where it becomes entangled or lodged in the minute cellular texture of that peculiar organ, causing centres for tubercular formations. Driftwood is likely to stop on the first obstruction in the river, and will accumulate more rapidly as the pile becomes extended and the force of the current abates: so of tubercles in the lungs. They generally begin in the upper part of the lungs, where the blood first enters, and increase more rapidly as the current of life ebbs away.

The first described condition is called the incipient stage of consumption, and is indicated by dry skin with unnatural surface heat, loss of flesh, and a dry, hacking cough, which advances to raising a glossy, viscid sputa—and here I will say, if physicians understood integumentary respiration, and what the brain battery is demanding for assistance in its efforts to re-establish surface respiration, the disease would never reach the second stage In the second stage the cough is deeper, the sputa heavier, chest sorer, with poorer appetite and respiration much more enfeebled. The third stage is attended with paroxysms of very severe coughing, the veins on the back of the hands become small and of a blue-black color, chills, hectic fever and night sweats follow, when the feet and ankles begin to swell with a dropsical clearness of the skin, the finger nails curl at the corners, loss of appetite, increased debility, with emaciation, diarrhœa sets in, and the patient dies from dyspnœa.

Consumptives have a tonic condition of the skin. Physicians have sought to relieve this condition by hot and cold water baths; also by sudorific treatment, not being aware of the real cause, the absence of the sebaceous lubricator. The effect of oil and of water upon leather is very different—the former softens permanently, while the latter soon leaves the article harder than before.

There has been an inexplicable puzzle about the chill, fever and colliquative sweats, from the fact that the electric motor and recuperative forces of the system have not been understood.

"What is a chill? It is a rigor. What is a rigor? A chill." That is as clear as mud.

When the scales of the cuticle are shut down, closing all the windows to the external world, the dictates of the cerebellum sends a large charge of electricity to the surface to skake the integument for the purpose of arousing the dormant circulation. This shaking is the rigor and the cause of the heat that follows, called the fever. Fever at the surface is always the result of electric effort. Electricity is the master workman sent by the battery to take the initiatory steps which are the indications of disease. Large expenditures of electricity produce exhaustion and sleep. In this condition the whole muscular structure is relaxed, all the minute sphinctives, closing the fluid capillaries and sweat pores, give way, when the surplus moisture exudes in what is familiarly called night sweats. The electric exhaustion caused the debility, and the debility set the fluids free which could not escape by evaporation from the morbid condition of the skin. I feel well assured that the profession is not prepared to understand the deleterious results arising from a suppression or loss of the sebaceous humor. Not having been taught anything about surface respiration or electric effect, how can they accept it? Not knowing the cause of a continued heat on the surface, resembling a slow fever, how could they find a remedy?

The method of treating consumptives has mostly consisted in the administration of expectorants and tonics. They have been given single, and compounded in every possible shade and grade, usually covered with sugar or honey, bottled up as a new and wonderful specific for all ages, stages and conditions of consumption, labeled "the latest discovery and only sure cure." The drug stores are full of these nostrums, which all fail, as does, also, the regular practitioner. During a long period of time consumption has been regarded as the incurable disease, both by the profession and the people. There is not an upstart seventeen years old, male or female, who has not learned to say, "I don't believe, when consumption is fairly seated, that it can ever be cured." They do not know what idea they are trying to convey by "fairly seated," nor where in the numerous departments of the human mansion this king of terrors has located his chair.

All consumptives can be cured in the first and second stages, excepting that class of people who, like July apples, are destined to decay before the winter of life sets in. Such persons generally have a long, slim neck, a small base brain, narrow chest, and thin face at the back part of the under jaw. Such persons are languid in disposition, mild, involuntary, electric battery weak, and powers of resistance small—ma's dear, dead pet, the kindest, mildest best child in the whole family.

The work of the historian is to deal with the dead past; that of the medical progressionist with the living present and a hopeful future. The question is not, how did we find out what is known?—but, how will we reach the unknown?

The brain not only furnishes electricity for all the voluntary and involuntary functions of the body, but also for its own action and volition. Thought is produced by action or motion of some part of the brain. To learn one thing, we must train the brain to make one movement. If we know many things, the brain must have been trained to make just as many different movements. These trained movements, united into groups, produce ideas; arranged in parallel lines of contrast, they produce what we call reason. So wonderfully is the brain constructed, that it is capable of almost an infinite number of movements by its action and counter-actions, involutions, evolutions and contortions. The method by which new truths are discovered and the sciences advanced is by grouping a combination of brain movements together. different from what had ever been arranged before, producing a new thought. This new unknown thought or pull of the brain is compared to and with a known thought or pull, or combination of pulls, resembling it, or the reverse of it, and the resemblance or contrast measured, which results in a new conclusion. Memory consists in the retentive power of the brain to reproduce a former movement or combination of movements. The first general brain movements of youth are coarse and large, like rocks in a field, and are easy to be found. As age advances and education develops the peculiar words of each branch of science and the truths they contain, greater complication and finer movements are required, resembling the smaller stones, pebbles and sand that make up part of the soil, which is itself composed only of finer particles. Therefore, the less a person knows, the oftener he repeats it and the sooner he can find it. Memory is method, order of the brain, capability of so arranging each link of a chain of ideas in such a manner that the last end of each brain pull is the first end of the next. A great many of the medical theories of the present day have emanated from men who never knew what it is to have a new pull of the brain. They are simply repeaters, from Hippocrates to Asclepiades, to Democritus, to Themison, to Thesalus, to Arelius, to Aretaus, to Archegenes, to Galen. Then came Paracelsus, the first man bold enough to administer mercury internally, and to entail upon his followers the epithet of destructionists. From him to Lydenham, to Watson and to Chambers; all quoting and repeating.

Begging pardon for what seems to be a digression, I will say, in the treatment of this disease the great work to be accomplished is to restore the skin to its normal condition, the sebaceous glands to their normal functions, and the skin, kidneys, liver and lungs will carry away all foreign and effete matter, thereby preventing all tubercular supplies. Oxygenize the blood through the skin, and under no circumstances counter-irritate the chest by the use of croton oil or blisters. Open your clogged sewers through the integumentary walls of the citadel of life, and let the filth flow into the ocean of space.

TREATMENT.

Clothing.—Patients should be clad like laboring people, avoiding all chamois skin wraps, heavy flannel bundles around the neck and chest, which shut off the fresh air from contact with the skin.

Exercise.—It is an axiom in consumption, "the stiller she lies the faster she dies." *Exercise!* EXERCISE! EXERCISE! Patients feel languid and desire to sit or lie down to rest. Movement makes them cough, and the cough is their greatest alarm, while in fact the cough is of the least account. They keep so still that the least movement hurts them. Spread down quilts on the carpet and make them roll over and over frequently, walk, swing, go up and down stairs, ride, etc. Encourage better voluntary breathing. All must be done with an eye to the ability of the invalid.

Diet.—The more milk the better. Let the patient have all the good food his appetite requires, without spices of any kind.

All the above will not cure a consumptive. Add the following, and they will :

Take one pound of clean, fresh lard, add one tablespoonful of water, in which has been dissolved a piece of anotto (annotto) as large as a pea, work them together till the lard is changed to a red shade. At bed time cause the patient to be rubbed with this lard from the bottom of his feet to his ears as thoroughly as he can stand. If he coughs periodically give him a dose of an excellent cough remedy* one hour before the exacerbation. Give the patient a long night dress. Grease and rub him every night till he has been treated five times. On the sixth evening wash him with castile soap in warm water, rubbing him thoroughly with a dry towel. Then treat five times as before and so on.

Why use lard in preference to any other oil? Because it is the nearest like the sebaceous lubricator, and because it absorbs oxygen with the greatest avidity, and because it leaves no coating, and because it cures.

Why rub the patient so thoroughly? Because it facilitates the circulation of the skin, and stirs up the thoracic and abdominal viscera, and imparts the electric vitality of the strong, healthy operator to the invalid.

---

* AN EXCELLENT COUGH REMEDY.

Tincture of bloodroot,	⅛ ounce.
Balsom of fir,	⅛ "
Oil of tar,	⅛ "
Alcohol,	1 "

Put in pint bottle, let it stand for two hours, shaking occasionally, until the alcohol has cut the balsom Then fill up with New Orleans molasses. Dose, one-half teaspoonful three times a day.

D. W. ELDERKIN.

1870.

IS THERE A SUPREME BEING;

AND DOES MAN POSSESS AN IMMORTAL INTELLIGENCE?

There is a class of philosophic progressive minds, who in their endeavors to wipe out error, superstition and priest-craft, and shed the glorious light of truth broadcast over an ignorant, benighted humanity, that have leveled their artillery against the belief in a supreme, omnipotent, omniscient and omnipresent God. The motives that prompted this investigation and warfare, without doubt, were good; but I know of no better way to judge of the merits of a conflict than by its results.

If these zealous progressionists could succeed in their effort to exterminate the belief in a supreme intelligence, whence comes the exalted excellence of the conquest? Who is made wiser or happier? Will the sun shine any brighter or warmer, or the rainfall be any more regular? Will planets and systems be better guided in their orbits, or nature be clad in a robe of greater attraction and beauty? If no good results, then the victory would be a failure.

Will they succeed? Can they succeed? Never! Their own arguments blot out nature and destroy universal law. The atheist reasons without revelation, I propose to answer him in the same manner. He says God could not make himself out of nothing. Suppose he could not; does that prove that he does not exist? Planets, suns and universes could not make themselves out of nothing, yet they exist in the sight and consciousness of all living intelligence.

Atheist replies, universes always existed. Why did not God always exist as well? He says God cannot be omnipresent, for space has no bounds, no limit, and God cannot be large enough to fill a space that has no outside or circumference. By what law can he determine that space is infinite and intelligence finite? Can the inferior limit the superior? Can the worm fix the bounds of the philosopher's mathematical scope? He says God cannot have form, for there would be no outside to him, consequently he cannot exist. Stop a moment, Mr. Atheist; has space an outside to it? and do you claim it does not exist on that account?

God may have a definition for form and space that the atheist does not find in his philosophy, and be adapted to both, and that adaptation no more incomprehensible to man than a space without limits, an eternity without beginning or end or a universe that was never made. It is impossible for finite reason to determine what the infinite cannot be or do. We find in nature a great unlimited intelligence, and that intelligence can only be measured by us with the capacity of mind that man possesses. When we examine a machine adapted to a special purpose, we say, what a complete design! What a perfect plan! Who was the inventor? Here we immediately seek the relation between the maker and the thing made, the plan and the planner, or the design and the designer. If we find a plan there must have been a planner. The locomotive, with its engine, boiler, carriage and couplings cannot be the result of an accidental falling together of wood and iron. Neither can it be formed by the inherent vibrations of atoms pulsating the molecules in the wood and metal, nor by the force of electric attraction and repulsion. Nothing but that power of mind, reason and skill, arising from a slight resemblance of those attributes ascribed to God, could plan and complete that machine. We judge the inventor's power of mind by the magnitude of his work; his wisdom by the complication and perfection of his production; the extent of his control over elements by his ability to adapt them to his purposes, and his goodness by the beneficent purposes accomplished. A philosophic atheist sees a plan in every department of nature; he sees also a planner, but is unwilling to call it or him God. He seeks for names or actions, like electricity, chemical attraction, involution and evolution, molecular force and atomic vibrations, anything except God. Every one of these elements or motions is as inexplicable to him or by him as the invisible God of the universe. Whatever we may call that great universal intelligence, He has displayed all through nature a system of machinery as much superior to a locomotive as eternity is superior in duration to one hour clock time. Look at the millions of suns in our universe with their primary and secondary planets, all held with unerring certainty in their orbits by a great plan of attraction and electric repulsion, displaying itself in the laws of centrifugal and centripital forces. Without the law of attraction planets and suns would break from their moorings and dash off through space in chaotic confusion. Without the law of electric repulsion the countless millions of orbs would fall together in one consolidated mass. In this great scheme of the universe every planet has its motion and its time, and its area of space to pass over in certain time. By the fulfilment of every part of the plan perfect order is maintained. We cite attention to God's plan of watering the producing surface of our earth. The world is surrounded by a very light, elastic atmosphere, composed principally of oxygen and nitrogen gases. This atmosphere, or the air that we breathe, is set in motion, causing wind, by three distinct methods—the attraction of the moon, the change in locality of electricity and heat, from the sun and other minor causes. This atmosphere, though several hundred times lighter than water, is used as the vehicle to buoy up and carry it all over the surface of the earth. Water, so essential to vegetable and animal life, is composed of oxygen and hydrogen gases, so combined that heat and motion separate and rarify them until they become lighter than the lower or evaporating stratum of the atmosphere, which varies from one to three miles in height. These gases ascend to the condensing or rain-forming stratum, where they are reunited into clouds. mists and showers, which are poured down upon the thirsty earth to renew and invigorate its vital forces. A portion of it is absorbed into the ground, whence it makes its way to the surface again in the form of springs, for constant use, flowing down by the law of gravitation in brooks, creeks and rivers to the level of the ocean. Who, of earth's engineers, can invent such a plan? Yet plan it is, containing a degree of divine intelligence so far superior to man that he can only see that it is done, without comprehending why or how any of these laws, with such definite certainty, complete their work.

Atheist talks of electric attraction and repulsion as creative agents, without knowing what causes the attraction or changes it to repulsion. He refers to the organizing and disorganizing capabilities and intelligence of matter, without knowing what mind is, or how it exercises the power of contrast or conclusion. He enlarges upon the motor power of matter, while he cannot define the power by which he moves himself. Still he knows all about how God cannot live, move or have a being. "He cannot live because He has no form, and because He could not make Himself out of nothing, and because He is of no use to a universe that can control itself without a God." "He cannot move because there is no God to move, and it would take Him so long to go the rounds of infinite space that the universe would all be left without a God." "He cannot have a being because He cannot fill unlimited space, and if He could, He could not occupy all space, for suns, planets, comets and aerolites occupy a portion of it, and his body would be riddled and every bone broken by swift-shooting meteors and revolving orbs." Such conceptions of God are only a reflection of man's own image, attributes and character. This process of god-making clothes each man's diety with all the vices, passions and malice which he may possess. When the atheist discharged his artillery it was aimed toward the Great Eternal instead of the host of reflected images, and the conflict is like the battle between the giant and Jupiter, "when the giant threw a hundred rocks against the planet at one throw, but Jupiter defeated him with thunder and buried him under Mount Etna." The Deity has any quantity of thunder, but the atheist lacks rocks.

God's plan of human happiness and eternal progression is a great puzzle to an atheist. He cannot comprehend that this life is a school in which that spark of immortality which is clothed in an earthly form and individualized by a conscious identity is taught by contrast and comparison to appreciate all that is lofty, noble, bright, glorious, truthful and lovely, from its lessons of good brought into contrast with evil. Though evil exists, it is only in quantity and quality sufficient to make the contrast complete. Our days of health, hope and happiness are many compared with their contrasts. The hours of pain, hunger, grief and pinching want are only a small fraction of an average lifetime. There is a motive in every intelligent action. Can matter, alone, without a God, plan a world where all its living creatures enjoy a thousand pleasures to one pain? Why would not the forces of matter be just as likely to reverse the conditions and erect an order of beings in which every sound would be a lamentation or shriek of horror, every sight a terror, every touch a deadly sting, every taste the bitterment of gall and every smell the stench of the valley of hades? Where love would be transformed into hatred, friendship into dire conflict, hope into wailing despair and humanity into a race of skeleton fiends. Or if matter was always on the better side, giving man a momentary temporal life, what motive did Mother Matter have in mingling his cup of happiness with the slightest tincture of misery? By the plan of that great Infinite Intelligence who never errs in His control over all his works, the spiritual part of man, by means of his physical form, is brought into direct contact with the laws of matter. His five senses are the media through which the spirit is brought into tangible relation with other beings and things outside of himself, which belong to material nature. In this world the lessons of eternal progression begin. If we neglect to improve this opportunity for the study of matter and God's laws, as manifested in its changes and wonderful displays of grandeur and beauty, we may suffer a fearful loss when we find ourselves removed to a higher department, that we are not qualified to enter. "But," says the atheist, "your spiritual being and immortality is all a humbug." The man who has darkened his hope of immortality and smothered the dictates of the spirit within, may exclaim humbug! when he has been driven from organization as the origin of life and knowledge, to electricity, and from electricity to chemical attraction, thence to molecular force, then to atomic vibrations, and finally to involution and evolution, which is nothing more than electric attraction and repulsion, and has been unable, with all his named forces, to explain one principle of inherent knowledge in any of them.

A man may deny the existence of an immortal principle within himself, and labor to attribute the varied phenomena of his spiritual nature in the body or out of it, to as many causes as he can invent, yet the irresistible conviction rushes back upon his rationality that he has an undying spirit within that moves and controls his body, and when out of it moves, dictates and controls itself. The atheist speaks of the mind of man. What does he mean? Organized matter, certainly! Matter must be a wonderful being, having mathematical powers almost unlimited, possessing philosophical capabilities to criticise and trace the laws of a universe, hope and aspirations that grasp eternal duration and a longing for immortality and eternal life. Its affections for parents and children are stronger than death. It loves the beautiful, progress in knowledge, and sympathizes with those who suffer. Do plants, trees, and rocks compute their distance from the sun or comprehend their relation to other matter? Do they weep when a twig or pebble is broken? All matter is permeated with spirit, but matter itself is not spirit. Man has a spirit. but he is not all spirit. The two elements—form and intelligence—are united in him for the purpose of organizing an individuality—a self-acting identity. They continue their union until intelligence is moulded into a consciousness of its own being and power, when it drops the perishable form, but retains its immortal form. Man's attributes, reason, love, hope, knowledge and sympathy are elements of the soul. If these elements cannot die, how can the spirit, which is the embodiment of them, die?

If Mother Nature is all there is of form and knowledge, producing and destroying in one everlasting succession, she is nothing better than an old harlot, strangling her offspring as fast as she gives them life and hope. But a higher power has pictured in man's bright imagination and noble reason a far away realmw here kindred spirits will re-unite and hail each other with the songs of the free; where parents will greet their children that were snatched from their tender embrace, and children will clap the glad hands of their dear old father and mother on that waveless ocean of eternal progression. Is the great God of worlds and systems and universes false to himself and his creatures? Is He a cheat and a deceiver? Will he plant the seeds of a tree that will never grow; cause a flower to germinate that can never blossom, or light up a hope of immortality in man's bosom that shall never be realized?

Why is there so strong a desire for knowledge; for the onward and upward progression? If at the dissolution of the body knowledge shall cease, hope and life cease, all that moves the body to activity, all that awakens the heart to sympathy and love, all that inspires the soul to adoration and reverence shall lie down in dark and silent oblivion. No, no! Man's spirit is a spark from the Great Eternal Life, and is immortal, else His existence is a discredit to unlimited wisdom and power, a cheat to Himself and an abortion from the bowels of nature.

If my atheistic friend could write this moment with the finger of destiny upon the broad canopy of heaven the astounding proclamation, that man lives only to die and live no more, what a universal wail would rend the air the length and breadth of our fair world! What blighted hope would wring the hearts of mankind! What unavailing tears would scald the withered cheeks of humanity, doomed to a death of eternal unconsciousness.

Oh! how cold and dark and blighting is that grave that covers all we are and hold dear in silent oblivion! Hark! a voice within, the whisperings of a higher life, assure us that we are immortal; that this life is only the stairway to our higher and nobler destiny. Good thoughts, words and deeds polish ourselves and brighten the pathway of others through the pilgrimage of this life. Seeking after wisdom and cultivating a hope of immortality and eternal life elevate our nature, expand our affections and bring us nearer the exalted realms of blessedness, purity, truth and light.

D. W. ELDERKIN.

Spartansburg, Pa., 1887.

INDEX.

In the following index the figure following the number of generation indicates the page whereon the name of the person appears in the family record of his or her parents. The second number gives the page where the record of that person's family appears. And the third number gives the page where the biographical sketch of the person may be found. The names of the women who married into the family appear but once in the index, the name after marriage being given. The names of women belonging to the family, who were married, appear twice, being indexed by their maiden name and by their name after marriage, in which case the maiden name is enclosed in parentheses, as seen in that of Fanny (Elderkin) Baker, whose name appears among the "B's" and "E's." Where they are indexed by their maiden name their name is followed by that of their husband, prefixed by an m.

By carefully noting the above it will be seen that the full record and lineage of any person can be traced accurately and easily.

www.ingramcontent.com/pod-product-compliance
Lightning Source LLC
Chambersburg PA
CBHW030359270326
41926CB00009B/1187